MW01094224

HERE'S WHAT SHATTERING B.

"Dolores took her experience as a professional coach and her wisdom as a woman and put together this magnificent guidebook which assists others who are on their personal journey to success how to overcome obstacles, set aside fear, burst through barriers and make the impossible, possible."

— Tracy Repchuk, Bestselling Author of
31 Days to Millionaire Marketing Miracles

"Dolores hits a home run with this book, giving the reader very specific tips and ideas to lead a more successful and joyful life. Her real time interviews are interesting and truly bring the real world to each segment. Buy it today not only for yourself, but for people in your life that need direction on living life to its fullest!"

— Marsha Petrie Sue, MBA, Author and Professional Speaker

"*Shattering Barriers* is a must read for women of all ages. The inspirational lessons shared can be life changing. Pick up a copy for yourself and every woman you care about empowering!"

— Debbie Allen, International Business Speaker,
Best-Selling Author and Motivational Film Star

"I've been riveted to every word like superglue. This information that Dolores has managed to capture and release so concisely smacks of vision, courage and transformation. Truly enlightening and sure to boost any woman serious about her business."

— Marie O'Riordan, International Media Specialist,
Former CNN Journalist Who Did Mother Teresa's Final Interview

SHATTERING BARRIERS

Amazing Women's Journeys
to Personal Empowerment

Dolores Seright

SHATTERING BARRIERS:
Amazing Women's Journeys to Personal Empowerment

By Dolores Seright

Printed and published in the United States of America

By Passport To Your Dreams, LLC

First Edition: September, 2011

ISBN 978-0-9838058-0-9

This book is dedicated to my loving husband, Jim King, whose support and love has never wavered, and to the women whose lives will change when they learn to believe.

YOU are as unique as the cloud formations that constantly change with the winds. Your uniqueness is an inherent part of who you are. I encourage you to discover your uniqueness, live your dream and love your journey. Your personal empowerment will come with your belief.

Dolores Seright

ACKNOWLEDGMENTS

My heartfelt thanks go to each of the women who bared their souls in the stories they have shared. They did this, not for themselves, but for the women who will read this book and believe that they can have a better, more fulfilled life because of what they have read and learned.

I want to thank my sister, Janet Schmidt, for her invaluable insight and suggestions when this manuscript was still an unpolished work. Her contributions made it possible to see the light at the end of the tunnel.

A special thank you goes to my daughter Jennifer, who is my creative resource. It is always an inspiration for me to see her genius at work, knowing that I did not encourage her to pursue her artistic dreams as a youth.

I am particularly grateful to my husband Jim, for his patience and support as I became an author.

I want to express my appreciation to my parents for always believing in me and encouraging me to follow my dreams.

Finally, I want to say how much the support of the family members and friends who believed in me and encouraged me to publish this book has meant.

INTRODUCTION

Are you a female who wishes there were more to life than the one you are living right now? If the obstacles seem overwhelming and the challenges never ending, do not give up hope, thinking that a life of quiet desperation is your fate. If you had dreams that have gotten lost somewhere in your journey to today, this book is for you. *Shattering Barriers* will change the way you think and provide resources you can use immediately. You will learn the powerful skills you need to energize your business, your career, and your life!

After reading this book, there will be no excuses.

This is not a typical business book. This is an adventure story. The stories you will read are *real life* examples of real women. They faced obstacles and challenges that many people cannot begin to imagine. They learned valuable lessons along their personal journey that they are now sharing with you. One of these stories will touch your heart and help you believe.

As you read their stories, open your heart and mind to the message being shared. Human beings are unique in that we frequently learn best the lessons from our personal experiences. My hope with this book is that you will recognize yourself in one of these stories and understand that the choices you've made put you where you are. The choices you make in the future can create a more successful future. You must only learn the skills.

CONTENTS

SECTION III
What's Holding You Back from Reaching Your Potential? .. 151

SECTION IV
Your Journey Begins Here 213

SECTION I

EXTRAORDINARY WOMEN IN EVERYDAY LIFE

"Life is not easy for any of us. But what of that? We must have perseverance and above all confidence in ourselves. We must believe we are gifted for something and that this thing must be attained."

—Marie Curie

EXTRAORDINARY WOMEN IN EVERYDAY LIFE

As I developed the message I wanted to convey in this book, I realized the value of including the stories of other successful women. These women may not be on the cover of *Time Magazine* or *Fortune 500 Company* CEOs, but these women are very successful in the career or business they chose. You encounter them every day, but may not recognize them. They don't wave their success in your face, saying, "Look what I've accomplished!" They live their success through helping others and living empowered lives. They discovered their own unique qualities and incorporated them into their personal style and into their business or career. The lessons and wisdom they share gives insight to women living in today's world facing the same challenges you face.

As I identified and interviewed remarkable women who had attained success, I discovered common threads. The journey each amazing woman traveled was often not a direct path to success. In most cases, each woman overcame huge obstacles, disappointments, or failures in her life or business before achieving her success. Their vision for their future was not always clear; in fact, often their early career or life meandered without focus. What they shared was an amazing journey, unique to each of them and the people they touched. These amazing women shattered barriers as they became who they are today. They each leave a legacy that lives on in the lives of those they touch.

My personal path of discovery was neither smooth nor well-marked. After completing high school, I followed in my mother's footsteps and become a secretary. I had the skills and had no desire to be a teacher or a nurse. My dreams were simply not big enough at that time to think beyond getting a job, getting married, and caring for a family. My first job was with a major pharmaceutical company as a secretary. I was excited to be earning a paycheck and loved learning how new products were discovered and brought to market. I learned quickly and was very good at my job. Soon I had an opportunity to work directly for a department manager and loved the experience. This position was many years ago when it was uncommon to see women in executive positions in the corporate world. I will never forget a comment that my department manager made to me during this time. He planted a seed that changed the course of my life and career. He said, *"It's too bad that the company doesn't hire female managers, because I think you would be a good one."*

I didn't know at the time how powerful those words were and the impact they would have on my life.

So how does this glance into my past help you find your own unique skills and talents?

Often the stories we read about other people and their experiences will trigger thoughts and memories of our own. As I share the stories of remarkable women with you, notice how their experiences prepared them for the next stage of their life or business. They made powerful

4

personal discoveries of their inner strengths and their unique skills or traits that enabled them to excel as they pursued new opportunities.

As I share these secrets through my journey and the journeys of many other successful women, you will learn techniques and skills that will result in success far beyond your current dreams. You will change your life, you will explode your business and your career, and you will achieve success beyond your wildest dreams!

"The future belongs to those who believe in the beauty of their dreams."
    —*Eleanor Roosevelt*

IT ALL STARTS WITH A DREAM

YOU are the author of your life story. The dreams YOU have and the choices YOU make will determine the ending. I challenge you to write the story you want to live. You are the star! Your journey will be yours alone. Who you touch, who you become, and the legacy you leave is unique to your journey.

Setting limits on your dreams prevents you from the success you desire in your business, your career, and your life. You may not even know you are doing it. Too often you listen to that inner voice say "you can't do that!" And you believe it.

What would you do if you knew you could not fail? You've heard this question before, but have you ever seriously answered it, if only to yourself?

"If you knew you could not fail . . ."

Powerful words. Believe them?

On a daily basis, we see failure all around us, and most of us have experienced failure in our lives. I believe this . . . the only true failure is when you do not learn from your past failures. Each and every failure you experience brings you closer to the success you desire if you evaluate and learn from the experience.

"If you knew you could not fail . . ."

7

Want to believe?

Remember, it's your story!

Dolores Seright Learned to Dream

Change your thoughts . . . change your actions! These six words can change your life forever. Many years ago I listened to a motivational speaker say, "You have, right now, exactly what you want in your life!" I was extremely upset to hear those words because I barely had enough money to pay the bills and buy groceries, and definitely had nothing left for the 'fun' things in life. How could this be true--I was working really hard at my job, rearing my children, and looking for a way to get ahead of the bills? But, I couldn't get his words out of my mind. If they were really true, I *was* responsible. Initially, I didn't want to accept that, but it was true. I was totally responsible. At that time, I didn't have the knowledge or the tools I needed. I stopped learning. I also stopped dreaming.

He continued talking about having dreams and dreaming BIG. I walked out of that meeting a changed person. I believed him, and my life was never the same!

I knew exactly what I needed to do, and I knew I had the secret in my possession to succeed in my career and my life.

To me, dreaming big meant exploring the world and expanding my horizons. I grew up in a small community surrounded by loving parents, brothers, sisters, and grandparents I visited frequently. Holidays always centered around boisterous family get togethers with aunts, uncles and cousins. We enjoyed the simple pleasures of picnics at the river and trips to see the exploding fall color of the leaves in the mountains. Working hard and doing your very best were lessons that were instilled at an early age. Each family member was charged with chores varying from washing the dishes, pulling weeds in the garden, or harvesting, canning, and freezing our fruits and vegetables for the winter months.

My first big "adventure" came when I was selected to attend a national Girl Scout Senior Roundup in Coeur d'Alene, Idaho. I was a junior in high school, and I traveled from Indiana to Idaho on a train packed with other Girl Scouts from states across the nation, all ready for fun and excitement. It was my first glimpse of the magnitude and beauty of our country, and I wanted to see more! I made a decision then and there to see our magnificent country, and today I have traveled to all but four states in the U.S. I had not yet learned about "goal setting," but I was already doing it.

"You can make $100,000 a year and more!" Don and Peggy Perryman were sitting at my kitchen table drawing circles on a piece of paper and discussing the Amway business opportunity. I had a high school education, was married, working as a secretary and caring for two children. The $100,000 seemed like a fortune to me, and I had never heard of multilevel marketing. It sounded pretty easy. Just buy the products and get your friends to sign up and do the same thing, right? That Amway experience changed my entire life. I quit my job to pursue it full time and went to every training program they offered. While I didn't make $100,000 in my Amway business, I learned skills and gained confidence that paved the way to my future success.

Finally, with $100 left in the bank, I found another job with a national security systems company. One day while working in their regional office, I remember saying that if I ever had an opportunity to move south and live by the water, I would do it in a heartbeat. Sometimes when you just put your desire out there, the universe puts situations in motion that help you get there. I received a phone call one day from a manager in this security company who was moving to Corpus Christi, Texas, to open a new branch office. We had worked together, and he remembered my comment that I wanted to live by the water. My husband and I traveled to Corpus Christi to check out the area, and I interviewed for the opening. A short time later we moved to Texas, and I began helping get this new office up and running. I also joined organizations and attended meetings to establish our corporate presence in the community.

At this time I never considered a career in sales; I was shy. But my boss observed a unique quality in me which was the ability to talk to people and make them feel comfortable with me and trust me. He knew that all highly successful sales people have that skill. I did not recognize that unique skill in myself, but I was open to input from someone I trusted. He convinced me that I could be successful selling commercial security systems, and I made a decision to take this new path in my career. I never entertained dreams of being a sales person. I did not think I had a sales personality. Little did I know at the time that I was about to discover that I loved selling. My future had just shifted.

One day, tired of wearing a hard hat on construction sites, I decided the time had come to look for a different type of sales position. More confident than ever before, I answered an ad for a pharmaceutical sales position. I got the job! I absolutely loved the industry and set sail on a new journey learning about diseases and medications and how they worked in the body. Through hard work and determination, I achieved success and moved up the corporate ladder, becoming a national trainer, a regional manager, a division director, and a then a regional business director. This was my dream career!

"*You have breast cancer!*" These were the most frightening words I had ever heard in my life. It was November 2005, and my life was transformed into a whirlwind of activity. Annual performance evaluations for the entire region were due. My husband and I were leaving for a much needed vacation in Tahiti. My life was BUSY! Those four words were life changing. I had a mastectomy in December and worked from home wrapping up company year-end projects. In January, I was back at work and attended the national meeting, conducting our regional sessions. Then chemo started. It was a common sight to see me in the chemo room working on my laptop, or off to the side of the room on a business conference call. Radiation treatments followed. My skin was so tender and inflamed at one point that my physician stopped treatments for a few days to allow it to heal. Four hours later I was boarding a flight to New Jersey for a director's meeting I had thought I was going to miss. Through the entire treatment regime I kept pushing forward, determined not to let the disease become my life. I had a life and goals and quitting just was not an option. That year, my region was number one in our division. My awesome team, I am proud to say, pulled together and made it happen!

At the end of the year, however, I knew it was time to change my focus and give myself time to heal physically and emotionally. I decided to retire and give back to my community. Knowing about a wonderful organization that helped empower women to get their lives back on track, I began volunteering as a career coach at Fresh Start Women's Foundation in Phoenix, Arizona.

Helping other women became my passion and sharing the sometimes sad but always inspiring messages of the women in this book is the fulfillment of my dream of encouraging others to believe and dream.

So is that it? Am I there? Have I accomplished my dream and my journey stops here?

Absolutely not! Once you learn to dream, and dream BIG, you just keep doing it. I want to combine my love of adventure with my passion and travel the country, even the world, if that is where the journey leads, helping other women to become empowered.

"If you're able to be yourself, then you have no competition. All you have to do is get closer and closer to that essence."
— Barbara Cook

WHAT MAKES *YOU* UNIQUE?

The first step is to *believe* that you are truly unique. No one else in the entire world is exactly like you. No one else has had your exact experiences or has your unique perspective in thinking, doing, and creating things. You see the world and its possibilities as only you can.

Have you ever really taken the time to think about what makes you unique and gotten to know that special YOU?

Remember the person that loved running, playing, and exploring? Or the person that loved enjoying the colors of the world around her? Were you maybe the person that loved to experiment, take risks, or try new things? Were you fascinated about learning how things worked? Were you curious about everything or maybe just loved math or reading?

All those things you loved as a child shape your future. Think about what was exciting and special to you before you began conforming to the rules of others in your life.

Did you pursue the things you loved? As you matured and experienced more of the world around you, what direction did your life take?

Did you follow where your heart led or were you influenced by others, setting your goals and dreams aside for a safer path? And today, what are the skills where you excel? What makes your face light up when you talk about it? What are you passionate about?

Answering these questions can help you identify what makes you unique. In later chapters, we will discuss why that uniqueness can be a key to your success in becoming a leader in your business or your career.

For now, know that it can be frightening to be different. You must create your own rules and forge your own path. You no longer follow others.

Remember Kermit's song, "It's Not Easy Being Green"? Well, it's not easy being unique, but it's worth it. You will have success and a special life of adventure unlike any others because it's *UNIQUELY* yours.

Let's begin right now discovering what makes you unique. The qualities that make you different, those causes you are passionate about, the activities that make your eyes sparkle and your heart sing, are all a part of your uniqueness that you can incorporate into your personal brand and leadership style. These qualities will shape the goals for your business, your career, your life, and your legacy.

Think back to your own childhood. Remember what your parents, grandparents and those close to you told you about that time in your life. Were you adventurous? Did you take things apart to see how they worked? Did you study people to see what they did or things to see how they worked? Did you daydream or imagine shapes in the clouds? Did you throw yourself into life or stand back and observe? Did you color outside the lines to see if it was okay to do so? Did you dance to music that only you heard? Did you sing until someone told you that you couldn't carry a tune? Or maybe you just hadn't had the training yet to develop the skill! Did you love learning new things? Were you a leader as a child? Did anyone ever tell you that you were really, really good at something? Did you run and jump into the swimming pool or maybe just splash around in the shallow end? Whatever you did was not right or wrong/good or bad. It is just a clue to you.

There is no better time than right now to take out a piece of paper and start writing down what makes you unique. Find a quiet place with no interruptions. Turn off your cell phone; forget email, texting and Facebook. You owe it to yourself to spend this time on you and your future.

This is the moment when many people will just skip this exercise. Why should I take the time to do this? I can just keep on reading and it will all make sense, right? I'm really too busy to actually do this. It won't actually change my life, so why bother.

I challenge you to be different. Take the time for yourself. Begin a journey that can put your life, business, and career on a path to greater success.

Childhood Dreams Are a Key to Your Uniqueness

• List all the activities you really loved to do as a child.

_____

_____

_____

_____

• Write down what you daydreamed about.

_____

_____

_____

_____

Now think about what you wanted to be when you grew up and write that down.

_____

_____

_____

_____

• Did that dream change over time? Write down all the things you ever wanted to be.

_____

_____

_____

_____

- List the comments family and friends said about you when you were young.

  _____

  _____

  _____

  _____

- As you are writing, remember what you got really excited about. Put it on your list.

  _____

  _____

  _____

  _____

- Review your list and just spend some time with your memories. These memories hold clues to your passions.

  _____

  _____

  _____

  _____

We will come back to this list later as we dig deeper into your unique qualities.

"It's not who you are that holds you back, it's who you think you're not."
— *Author Unknown*

SELF-ESTEEM:
IS YOURS AS HIGH AS YOUR GOALS?

Do you recognize your value as a unique individual here on our planet and that you can contribute something that no one else can? Self-esteem is the opinion you have of yourself. A simple definition, but your self-esteem powerfully impacts virtually every aspect of your life. Self-esteem not only influences your relationships and your career, but also the total of your accomplishments in life. High self-esteem makes it possible to function effectively. It allows you to take risks and make decisions about your life that are necessary to achieve a successful life.

Do you believe you can create a successful life? When your life is not going well, do you believe you can overcome the challenges you face? Do you deserve to be happy and successful? If you can emphatically say "Yes" to all three questions, you have healthy self-esteem. Not really certain you can overcome every challenge that comes your way? What you think of yourself and your abilities may have been influenced by events in your past. If you hesitated saying yes to any of these questions, consciously or unconsciously, those thoughts may still be holding you back.

Listen to what you say to yourself. Do you ever say, "I was stupid for saying that?" Or maybe you tell yourself, "I can't learn that; I'm not smart enough?" Or how about, "No one likes me because I'm unattractive?" What about, "I can't do it?" This self-limiting talk is programming your present thoughts and actions. If that inner talk is based on past beliefs, ask yourself if those beliefs were valid or if they were filtered through events and emotions that are no longer valid in your life?

Starting right this minute, pay close attention to your self-talk, and control what you say to yourself. The instant a negative thought comes into your mind, stop and ask yourself, "Why did I think that?" "Is it valid?" "What should I be thinking about myself and my abilities?" Keep awareness of your self-talk high and practice constantly. In a very short time it will become a habit and you will see the difference in how you approach your life. Your confidence will soar and your actions will be those of the unique, successful person you were always meant to be.

Learn the techniques of positive self-affirmations and implementing your personal action plan and watch your life soar to new heights!

Clarissa Burt's Self-Esteem Regime™

"I fight demons every day," were words I never expected to hear Clarissa Burt say. She has appeared on the covers of *Vogue, Cosmopolitan, Harper's Bazaar* and many other magazines, and has been a runway model for top designers from Chanel and Armani to Versace and Dior. Clarissa's face has been published on more than 250 magazine covers and her celebrity career has spanned thirty years. A picture of her during a private audience with Pope John Paul II has a treasured place in her office in Cave Creek, Arizona.

When I arrived at her home for our interview, Clarissa took me on a tour of her home. She had just started a garden in her backyard and was thinking about buying a composter. Her closet held more shoes than most women dream of, which were organized in bins in her closets with labels, but she lives in flip flops and remarks, "Who wears them?" Wrapped Christmas gifts set in a bedroom, telling me she shops the after Christmas sales to take advantage of the half-off prices, and I think about how all women love a bargain!

Clarissa had just spent days reorganizing her home. She needed a larger office able to handle the new business she was building. The family heirloom room, her past, had to be stored away to make room for her future.

"One of the most difficult things has been trying to figure out what I wanted to do next. Because I've had such a blessed life and I've been able to do pretty much anything I've wanted to do, and I've wanted to do a lot!" she shares.

But, if we rewind back to Clarissa's childhood, it wasn't quite as glamorous as it seems. Clarissa's mother was single when she got pregnant during the late 1950s. Coming from a staunch Irish Catholic family this was like a black mark on your soul, so these two young kids who had gotten themselves into trouble had to get married. Her father became an alcoholic, and Clarissa grew up in a home where there was a lot of violence and not many 'warm fuzzies.' "It was really tough stuff," Clarissa shared. "If I didn't get A's and B's, I was physically punished, but no one ever sat down to help me with homework." The firstborn of three, Clarissa knew most of her life she wasn't wanted, because she heard it all the time from her parents. The physical and mental regimen of punishment was very difficult and continued for years. By age sixteen Clarissa had developed

21

many health problems. She was also running the household by then, which meant doing dishes, dusting, and running the vacuum every single day. Friends could not come over and she and her siblings could not go out after school. There was never any time to have fun.

Growing up in New Jersey, Clarissa dreamed of going to New York City. Upon graduation from high school, she started looking for a job in the big city. Working with an employment agency, she went on a few interviews, but hadn't gotten a job yet. The agency told her they had just gotten something in, but she wasn't qualified. Determined and desperate for work, Clarissa convinced them to send her for an interview anyway. The position was with a high-end menswear company as an administrative assistant to an executive vice president and paid $25,000 a year. She got the job! She had to get up at 5:00 every morning, take the train and transfers and literally run the final blocks to get to the garment district and to her desk by 8:30. She laughingly tells me about stopping each morning for hot tea and a roll with butter, and losing weight from running to her job each morning.

Clarissa shares a story about her boss asking her one day if she could stay over in the city for a night. She says, "I really didn't get it about what I was going to be doing until he asked what kind of bubble bath I liked!" She said she was shaking when she called her mom for advice, already knowing what she would do. "I went into his office the next day and told him I didn't know what I had done to make him think I wanted to take a bubble bath with him, but I didn't; and if he wanted me to resign, I would get my things and go. He didn't and we never mentioned it again," she said.

By this time people were telling Clarissa she should become a model. She did not recognize her own beauty at this time. Her mother always disapproved if she saw Clarissa looking in the mirror, saying, "What are you looking for . . . the monkey to jump out?" Her mother disliked Clarissa's father or anyone telling her she was pretty. Today Clarissa recognizes that many of her own issues with low self-esteem were because of her difficult and stressful family situation.

Clarissa borrowed $300 from a coworker to have her test photographs taken. Taking them to Ford, Wilhelmina, and Elite Agencies, she was accepted by Wilhelmina and Elite. She chose Wilhelmina Agency and began working as a model, still unsure she could do it. Within a year Clarissa found herself in Paris where she worked for a year, describing those first years as "lean and meager, and often having bananas for dinner." Clarissa was not fond of Paris, and after a year she moved to Italy. "When you're a kid, you don't allow the fear to block you," she says. "I knew I had to follow my dream because it was stronger than I was, and when I got to Milan, my career took off almost immediately!" She stayed in Italy for 28 years as a highly successful print and runway model. She parlayed into television and then moved forward to start her own company, Clarissa Burt Productions, and she organized and launched the Miss Universe Pageant in Italy.

Clarissa talked about the experience of starting her first business. "When I opened my own company in Italy, it was really, really tough! I started a company thinking it would just take care of itself." She laughingly says, "I didn't realize you had to have strategies and marketing and capital, relationships and managerial skills. I just wanted to be Clarissa Burt Productions! In retrospect it was actually pretty exciting because in five years, I took Miss Universe from nothing to a three-hour-live broadcast in prime time with two thousand people sitting in a castle in Calabria, Italy. The productions I put on were mega-galactic, but so were the bills because I paid them. Sponsors weren't paying me, and there was so much to learn because the organization grew too fast. I learned the hard way and it was very costly. I think if I had paid for four years of university, four years of grad school, and four years of specialization, that's what I learned. You have to learn somehow. Business is tough and it's tough when you are a woman alone and you have celebrity status. Everyone thinks you are a gazillionaire! The work I did was amazing to someone looking from the outside, and there were so many cracks in the foundation. But I learned a lot."

Clarissa closed her business and left Italy to return to Arizona. Drained physically, mentally, and emotionally, she took the first year off. She didn't want to think about what was next. She just wanted to chill out, have fun with her family, and spend time with her grandmother. The two years which followed were spent in a disastrous relationship with someone she calls 'the biggest shyster in the world.' Clarissa worked with him in his company doing startups and running operations. After her relationship ended, she shares that she went through a period of depression and had to deal with personal self-esteem issues. "I had some pretty dark moments and really had to pull myself back together," Clarissa said. It was time to move forward and by 2009, she began putting her life together and planning what she was going to do next.

Clarissa started to research business opportunities, saying, "I can sit at the computer for fifteen to eighteen hours a day for weeks on end! And I've done it just to figure out who I am and what I can do. I now know what I really want to do is teach women everywhere how to have a strong self-esteem."

"I've always worried about what other people think of me. I decided it really was time to get over that. That's a big problem with self-esteem . . . worrying about what other people think! I want people to know the real Clarissa Burt." She just launched *Clarissa Burt TV: Look Good, Feel Good, Be Good, Do Good*. It is starting with four videos and airing two times a month. The videos include amazing people with products and services to help you look better, feel better, be better, and give back. The focus of her message is positive self-esteem and helping women help themselves."

In the midst of planning her new business venture, Clarissa was asked to be on the Italian version of *Survivor*. She left for six months, spending a total of nine weeks as a contestant in Nicaragua. "It was more difficult than you could ever imagine. I was thrown out of a helicopter and almost broke my back. I was in the hospital for thirty-six hours. For nine weeks I was consumed by No-see-ums, tiny biting flies that live near the water. I scratched and will have scars on my body for the rest of my life. It was hotter than Hades and humid. I would go to bed . . . actually I would lie on the ground at night and put as much clothing on as I could. I am terrified of crabs and they were everywhere. Some were huge. I faced some of my biggest fears laying down at night not knowing where they were. You face your fears and you get over it and you learn what you are made of."

I asked Clarissa what she came out of there with and she laughed and said "a lot of money!" Clarissa did say that she learned a lot about trust and feels an important lesson for her was that she could only trust herself. Thinking she was building relationships and alliances which didn't hold up, was a difficult lesson. She placed fifth of twenty-five people.

Back in Arizona, Clarissa juggles the launch of *Clarissa Burt TV* with her other passions and interests. "One of my major goals is to get married in 2011. It's already June and I don't see it happening! I would love to be in a relationship and be happily married the rest of my life. I turned fifty-two recently and when you look at the next fifty-two years. . .," Clarissa's thoughts were looking to a future she is creating for herself.

She practices her personal '*Self-Esteem Regime*™', and she developed and teaches Personal Envelopment™. It is personal development through personal envelopment, *i.e.*, the love of self--wrapping yourself in love for yourself--because until that happens, nothing else is going to fall into place. Clarissa believes, "The most important relationship you are ever going to have is with yourself. Most people don't understand what that is and what it means."

"It really hurts me to see women in pain," Clarissa shared. She has worked with many young women to help them build their self-esteem, and she has even brought some of them into her home to help them out of bad situations until they were strong enough to face the world on their own. She truly believes in paying it forward and giving back.

Clarissa was asked by an organization in Italy to spearhead the campaign in the United States to have *Walking Africa* nominated for a Nobel Peace Prize. "How could I say 'no'?" The goal is to bring awareness and recognition collectively to African women who are the backbone of that continent. Hundreds of thousands of these women walk miles a day for food and water and endure unspeakable hardships. Yet, amidst their many challenges and responsibilities, they share a joy of living. Recently Clarissa spoke to the European Parliament in Brussels and the Department of Foreign Affairs in Italy about *Walking*

Africa. She is currently appealing to prominent African American women in the United States to gain support as she launches a campaign here for the *Walking Africa* nomination for the Nobel Peace Prize. Clarissa excitedly shared that she was just invited to blog for the *Huffington Post* about the *Walking Africa* campaign.

Clarissa's message is about "forgiveness and letting it go. That is the only way I could learn, and in the great master plan I was supposed to learn so I could teach and help others with self-esteem. I don't know how many I can help before the angels call me, but if I just help one . . . actually, I already have."

"Adversity has the effect of eliciting talents, which in prosperous circumstances would have lain dormant."

— *Horace*

OVERCOMING ADVERSITY

Our ability to learn from our life experiences is one of our human traits. Being fearful of doing something and still taking action teaches us to overcome our fears and become more confident in our approach to life. Most everyone will face adversity and obstacles at some point in their life. How we handle them is a choice we make. The decision to step up and face your challenges head on allows you to grow and learn from the experience. You will discover inner resources and skills that will be with you for a lifetime, and you will learn to trust in yourself and your ability to succeed.

Carina Prescott Is Fearless!

"I'm FEARLESS" is the description Carina used when asked how she describes herself. "I have a deep faith and know that with the next step, *I'll be there.*" When I asked her how she discovered her uniqueness, she said simply, "Someone told me."

I first met Carina at a Breakfast Club meeting in Phoenix. I received an email invitation to this event and decided to attend even though I didn't know anyone, including the person who sent the invitation. Carina was a longtime member and warmly welcomed me to the group. As I got to know Carina, I realized she was very special. She was highly successful in her business, adventurous, and currently exploring her own personal potential. People were drawn to her, as I was. The story she shared with me during the interview for this book is an amazing account of resilience and courage that would cause most people to falter, yet Carina emerged strong and absolutely determined to succeed.

Imagine growing up with parents who were addicts, as Carina's were. Her father disappeared from the family long ago. When Carina was twelve years old, her mother disappeared for three weeks. Carina found a job sweeping floors and stocking shelves in a convenience store just so she could buy food for herself and her younger brother. As a child, each day was only about survival. She learned to make good decisions--her survival depended on it. At age fourteen she was able to tell her mother, "No, you are not in charge. I am. I'm the responsible one." And at fifteen Carina left home to live on her own. School meant everything to her at this time, and she had the wisdom to hang out with good people who encouraged her until she graduated high school.

College, however, was not an option and Carina went to work at a bank, earning a salary of $250 a week. There, Carina met Elizabeth, who would become her lifetime mentor and friend. Carina explained, "Elizabeth was everything I wanted to be. She was a self-made millionaire, sophisticated, empowered, and a brilliant, creative woman. She was a 'mom' to me, and I modeled after her." Carina learned quickly and went from earning $250 a week to $80,000 annually. During this time and for many years to come, she still carried within her very strong feelings of anger toward her mother, and was determined to prove her own worth by becoming successful. Today, years later, she is able to say that she "celebrates her past and believes her mother was put on this earth to teach me how to love and how to forgive."

Carina met Matthew in 1987, and made a decision to leave the corporate world in 1995. She and Matthew became business partners and together they built a highly successful and unique appraisal business, Lucid Valuations & Investments. "You don't grow up wanting to be an appraiser," says Carina. "It's not glamorous." It might not be glamorous, but it does occasionally have interesting projects such as appraising the carousel, complete with zoo animals, for the Phoenix Zoo. One day while reading an industry magazine Carina noticed an advertisement for a training program which would allow her to specialize in the appraisal industry. She discovered her niche. "There are only eleven people in Arizona who do what I do." "Separate from the pack," she advises. "I did it. Most people aren't like me. They just don't do it." She loves being self-employed and says, "I'm unemployable. The corporate world would never hire me."

Carina *is* "fearless". She's not willing to settle, and one of the secrets to her success is seeing something and saying, "I want that!" When I asked her if she always knew she was going to be successful, Carina said, "Yes!" She often looked at catalogs and said to herself, "I'm going to have that someday." Her dreams of a life very different from her difficult childhood motivated her to continue learning outside of the traditional educational system.

Carina believes her greatest personal achievement is the adoption of her son, Cameron, one of the loves of her life. She had not planned to be a mom, fearing that she would be like her own mother. Overcoming this fear opened her to blossom as a mother, and she treasures the experiences of motherhood.

Carina advises every woman "to surround yourself with really powerful women who are not in competition with you, but uplift you and believe in you just the way you are, without judgment." The women Carina had surrounded herself with were supportive of her when she and Matt decided to end their marriage. "We did everything backwards," she described their separation and the dissolution of their marriage; they remained in business together thinking that would preserve their income and financial security. Carina did not realize how difficult this working relationship would become. She decided initially to move her office out of the business location and work from her home. The future of the business is still undecided, but she is exploring options and is excited about her next venture.

Carina tells me that she didn't realize how emotionally dead she had become. As her marriage was failing, her zest for her life and her business was dwindling. Today, there is a sparkle in her eyes and excitement as she shares a picture of a gentleman she met through www.match.com just as she was about ready to close her account and abandon her efforts to meet someone interesting. As she talked, I was reminded that as we face endings in life--which we all do--we must remember how precious new beginnings are.

Carina is passionate about life! She is also passionate about helping those less fortunate and gives generously to an organization that provides food to people in need. She remembers that little girl who had to find a way to feed herself and her brother.

Carina says "Do it! Go for it! Don't be afraid to live free and don't settle for anything less than greatness."

Carina has not yet lived her full dream. Recently she made an important decision to follow her own advice to begin designing and living her dream life.

What Obstacles Are You Facing?

Obstacles can be present in different degrees in more than one area of your life. The magnitude of the obstacle, as well as the area of your life it is impacting, makes it necessary for you to prioritize its importance. As you begin to evaluate what obstacles you are facing, consider the six major areas of your life. These areas include financial, professional, health, spiritual, emotional and relationships. List your obstacles below and rank their importance.

- My financial obstacles are:

- My professional obstacles are:

- My health obstacles are:

- My spiritual obstacles are:

_____

_____

_____

_____

- My emotional obstacles are:

_____

_____

_____

_____

- My relationship obstacles are:

_____

_____

_____

_____

"The minute you alter your perception of yourself, both you and your future begin to change."
— *Marilee Zdenek*

YOU CAN CHANGE YOUR CIRCUMSTANCES

Remember hearing the saying, "Necessity is the mother of invention." It might not be true in every instance, but not being happy with the circumstances in our lives can definitely become the incentive to start thinking creatively about how we can improve our situation. Just taking the time to look at your life, your business, or your career from different perspectives and discover little opportunities that we can fulfill may be all it takes to discover an undeveloped talent or skill. When you put your unique touch into it, doors open and you are on the way!

Dana Morgan-Hovind's Unique Path

Dana Morgan-Hovind's discovery followed the birth of her first child. Dana had never dreamed of owning her own company or designing a clothing line for boys. When I first met Dana, she was totally focused on advancing her career in the pharmaceutical industry. She was a person you noticed immediately when you walked into a room. Dana was very tall, attractive, with a fantastic sense of style. But it was her personality that electrified the room. Dana truly lives every moment of

37

her life to the fullest. She totally immerses herself in the moment whether at work or at play. Dana describes herself as, "driven, creative, and passionate." She says, "I was raised to believe that I can do anything I want if I want it bad enough, and that there is nothing between me and my goal except air and opportunity."

Finding her niche was not her priority when she left her corporate job for a three-month maternity leave following the birth of her first son. "I just could not imagine ever working like I had been. My first day back to work was a five-day overnight meeting in Atlanta. It was this meeting where I changed my career path and direction. All I could think about while at the meeting was how I just wanted to spend this time with my son. I did not want to travel 75% or more of each month. My husband was a huge support. The day I told him that I wanted to be a stay-at-home mother, he said, 'if you really want to do this, we will figure out how to make it.' " After a few months of staying home, Dana's entrepreneurial instincts surfaced and she realized there were very few stylish clothing options for boys. While shopping in the malls and boutiques, searching for clothing for her new son, Dana was struck with the thought that she could design and create a hip and cool style that she would want to buy for her son and other infant and toddler boys. "Three months after becoming a stay-at-home mom, I tell my husband that I need to wire 'a carload of money' to China so that I can get the shirts and blazers that I just created. He never held me back or questioned what I was doing, and '*d mo baby*' was launched."

"Absolutely, yes, I took risks," said Dana. "Going into the apparel market was very tough, and the scariest part of starting my business was when I wired an enormous amount of money to China, not knowing if I would receive what I had designed and ordered. The second scariest part was when my shipment was in route from China, and I had no idea how I was going to get it into the buyer's market."

A vision of a unique clothing line for little boys, a strong belief in herself, and the ability to accomplish what she set out to do sustained Dana during one of the greatest challenges she ever faced. The customs agent held her entire shipment because the manufacturer forgot to place care labels in the zip ties. By now, Dana was nine months pregnant with her second son and was forced to go to the sweltering customs warehouse and sew labels into 1000 zip ties. These labels still didn't meet the standards of the customs agent. Dana did this three times before the shipment, which was accruing daily storage charges, was released.

Asked about her uniqueness, Dana says it is, "an uncanny ability to tackle things outside of my comfort zone. I am always looking for opportunities . . . not waiting on them to appear." I was reminded of the importance of our individual responsibility as role models when Dana said she figured out her unique abilities when, "It was ingrained in me as a child." One of her memories is of her father handing her a set of brakes for her car and telling her to install them. Another is when she sent letters to colleges in hopes of being awarded an athletic scholarship.

Dana believes, "Nothing is impossible!" She witnessed several of her designer friends close or sell their businesses when the recession hit, and she watched other boutiques close their doors. Her fashion line actually grew 23% during this time. Dana's defining moment came during her first apparel market show when she witnessed the clothing she had designed on models walking down the runway as she watched the buyers' reactions to her line. "It was unbelievable," she says.

Dana's advice to female business owners and women climbing the corporate ladder: "Stay grounded. Don't lose who you are! Be agile and quick to adapt to oncoming challenges."

Being successful in your business or career requires that you acquire and develop leadership skills. Dana says, "Your abilities are what put you in the role of leadership; the way you use those abilities, and the actions you take are how you earn the respect of those you lead. A title does not give you leadership."

Winning in the success game will be different for each of you reading this book. While achieving unbelievable success in business, Dana's greatest personal success was marrying her husband and being blessed with the two most unbelievable boys a mom could ever wish for.

Remember that you define your success in business and in life, and you write the story.

"The whole secret of a successful life is to find out what it is one's destiny to do, and then do it."

     — *Henry Ford*

DISCOVER YOUR PASSION

Waking up each morning bursting with excitement, enthusiasm, and a zest for life sounds terrific, doesn't it. Can't wait to get up and start a new day doing something you love and loving what you are doing? Is this how you currently start each of your days? In fact, do you ever begin a day feeling excited? No, I'm not a Pollyanna; and, yes, I understand that some of you reading this book have spent a lifetime getting an education and building a career. And some of you really do not like what you are doing. If you are not really excited about your career or your life, understand and realize that you have choices. You might not be able to turn your life around in a day, but you can begin today to discover the direction you want to go next.

Miranda's Dream of a World with People Helping Others

Lights! Camera! Action! The red carpet is out and people are laughing and chatting. Everyone is excited about landing their spot in front of the camera. At the center, Miranda adjusts the clothing, hair, and makeup of celebrities before the photographer captures their photos.

Miranda's Red Carpet Extravaganza, an exciting event at major networking functions and product or business launches, is one of Miranda's specialties today. It wasn't always like that for her.

Broken dreams plagued Miranda, it seemed her entire life. At age two, her mother's emotional instability and illness was only the first in a series of events which impacted Miranda and affected her view of the world and her place in it. At age two, she didn't understand why she was taken to live in a foster home for two years. At age four, she went to live with her grandparents for a time. Then, four years later, Miranda unfortunately entered the social system, living with foster parents for many years to come. As Miranda got older, she learned that her mother, an intelligent woman, was emotionally damaged. Now a young teenager, Miranda recognized that support was available to her from her teachers and athletic coaches, and thought that if she were the 'best,' she would never be alone. When foster care stopped at age fifteen, she made a life-changing decision to join the Job Corps, and then earn her GED. This decision resulted in a major shift in both her life and her future outlook. Within six months she had secured a full scholarship to attend college where she also became a varsity cheerleader. Her prospects were definitely looking up. But the broken dreams touched her life once more when Miranda's mother again became seriously ill. Miranda quit college to return home and care for the mother she only lived with for a total of four years of her life. Her mother passed away when Miranda was twenty-five years old, but she had instilled some powerful beliefs in Miranda during these precious years. One of those lessons was to, "Get an education; no one can take away your education," her mother told her.

Miranda wants every woman to learn "not to believe everything anyone tells you." She learned this at age eighteen when talking to a Navy recruiter. She said, "I'll do anything but cook!" Six months later she was in the Navy and she was a cook. "I was very gullible," she says, "and my initial goal was to get my college degree and become an officer. Boot camp was tough. They take away your dignity, your beliefs, and your values, and yet, at the same time the military is building you up to defend your country without question. Upon graduation from boot camp, your mind is alert, your movements robotic, saluting anyone walking by, uncertain of what is next. Your job is to protect the freedom of your country . . . no matter what. But, I knew I would never be 'me' again; however, I was hoping I would be better." Her life experiences had not prepared her for life in the military.

Miranda married shortly after boot camp and became pregnant within six months. She thought she had found the family she wanted with her husband, their child, and the military. But married life in the military can be very difficult when spouses with children find themselves on different tours of duty. She asked for an 'early out' from the military, which was granted after serving her country for three and one half years. Her husband left her and their daughter, shattering her dreams of a happy family. She was now working at Wendy's as a manager with a two-year-old child and a newborn to support. Miranda had no help. Yet, true to her military commitment, she remained in the Active Reserves and then in the Inactive Reserves.

Her mother's advice to get an education, learn to type, and get into computers was crucial to the next step in Miranda's life. BDM International hired her because of her computer training and her Job Corps' certificate. They had a pilot program in New Mexico, where

Miranda was now living, which paid for day care. She was about to learn another valuable lesson. Her boss was extremely detailed and he really pushed her to excel in her job. He taught her, "details matter," and Miranda has used this lesson to her benefit in every subsequent endeavor.

An opportunity to move to Dallas and work for Western Union changed everything for Miranda. This job doubled her income to $40,000 annually, and she knew she could take care of herself. She went back to school and attained a Bachelor's Degree in Business Administration with a minor in Marketing. She was then introduced to sales. As with many women, Miranda never saw herself in that role. She was raised in a very rural, small community in New Mexico, and always expected to be a wife and mother, not a career woman. She accepted a position as an Enrollment Advisor with the University of Phoenix Online and was extremely successful in sales. With success came confidence, and with that newfound confidence, she approached the University of Phoenix with a plan to create and implement a program for military personnel into their curriculum. This program was both innovative and successful for the University of Phoenix.

Miranda's inspiration comes from her mother, who empowered her with the words, "You can be anything you want to be." When making decisions, Miranda always asks herself, "Would my mother approve?" Her mother told her "Do things that other people are not willing to do, and do them well." Though her time with her mother was very short in actual years, the impact upon her life was great. I asked Miranda if she always knew she was going to be successful and she said, "No, but my mother always told me that I would be."

Miranda's advice to women is to, "Listen a lot! I made the mistake of wanting to show what I could do and prove myself. I did not think I was worthy of asking for compensation commensurate with the skills I already had." She recommends that you trust yourself and your intuition, and if your gut is telling you it's good for you, remember to treat yourself in some way. She also wants you to ask yourself if your behavior is good for your children. When the chips are down, keep going and don't give up. You will get through difficult times because it will always get better.

When I asked Miranda about discovering her own uniqueness, she said, "I just thought I was weird. I was different, but I wanted to help people and I have the ability to find 'special' niches." This uniqueness and a desire to help local business people in Phoenix led to the founding of Miranda's KISS. Miranda laughingly asks, "Have you had your KISS today?" Keep Image Successfully Simple is her brand, and she helps people find and promote their unique niche.

Miranda also founded Media Pro Productions, where she provides opportunities for many interns to develop and use their skills to offer affordable media to small business owners. These interns gain valuable work experience to help them advance in their careers.

Miranda continued to pursue her education and has a Master's Degree in the field of special needs. Pursuing her personal passion, Miranda founded Circle of Helping Hands, a 501(c)(3) non-profit corporation whose advocacy team helps children and families, people with special needs, and veterans. Her team of advocates is 95% successful helping these people obtain their benefits or find employment. She wants Circle of Helping Hands to be her legacy. Her goal for people everywhere is to choose COHH as their favorite charity and recognize the invaluable help it provides to those in need of a helping hand.

What most people don't know is that Miranda is a disabled Veteran. She struggles daily to summon the wherewithal to fulfill promises, when even minor tasks take significant effort and strength. How does Miranda accomplish mentoring successful organizations? She surrounds herself with an incredible team of volunteers and interns. And the biggest surprise of all . . . no one asks to be paid. All services provide the tools to assist those who cannot help themselves, or afford the expenses of doing business. What do the many volunteers and interns receive? Work experience, camaraderie, knowledge about how to build a business of their own, enjoyment of community service, and the satisfaction of helping each other. A Veteran's social worker once told Miranda, "You are disabled . . . you are not dead!" These words play over and over in Miranda's mind, and when times get tough and she wants to quit . . . she remembers the words.

Paying it forward and understanding that one person really can make a difference is what Miranda is all about!

"Follow your passion, and success will follow you."
— *Arthur Buddhold*

LIVING YOUR PASSION

Enthusiastic, excited, motivated! Look at the energy! These are the words used to describe people living their passion and loving their life. Quit living a life of 'quiet desperation' and say, "I want that! I love what I do when I head out the door each morning." Or maybe you don't have to head out the door because you work from the comfort of your home. For those of you who really dream big, maybe your office is at the beach, or it moves from country to country with you as you travel and explore the world. The only thing holding you back is your openness to explore new possibilities.

Jyl Steinback's Passion for Teaching Healthy Habits

The President's Council on Fitness, Sports & Nutrition recently awarded Jyl Steinback the 2011 Community Leadership Award. Jyl exemplifies many leadership qualities as Executive Director of Shape Up US and "America's Healthiest Mom." She is also a cookbook and lifestyle author with fifteen-plus books to her credit that have sold over two million copies. The media describe her as "enthusiastic," "America's Super (Healthy) Mom," "a national sensation," "a one-woman business

47

dynamo," and "a weight loss guru." It all began through her role as a mother of two children. Jyl continues to demonstrate her commitment to the mission of helping others to become healthy.

Shape Up US is not the culmination of a lifetime's work, but another step in the journey Jyl Steinback has traveled since college. Upon receiving her Bachelor's Degree in Education from Arizona State University and teaching for a year, Jyl realized that rather than full-time teaching in a classroom, creating a program to teach children to live a healthy lifestyle gave her a sense of purpose. Her dream job at that time was to work for Elizabeth Arden in Beverly Hills, but a job opening wasn't available right then. She moved to Southern California to work for Golden Door Spa in Escondido, but within three weeks, she was offered her dream position in Beverly Hills. "You gotta go after your passion," Jyl exclaims! And she proceeded to do exactly that, becoming a personal trainer to the stars.

Continuing to pursue her passion for healthy lifestyles, when Jyl married and moved back to Arizona, she started Jump For Life, a cutting edge aerobic movement using mini trampolines. She admits the program was, 'before its time,' though mini trampolines are extremely popular today. Through her experience, Jyl realized that she preferred work that didn't involve confinement to a single location, but allowed her to reach out and help more people. In 1993, a friend suggested she write a cookbook to help complete the equation of a healthy lifestyle. "But I'm not a cook," Jyl replied. Undeterred, her friend convinced her that the winning combination of cooking for her family every day and her knowledge about health and nutrition would lead to success. It did, and she wrote and published her first cookbook.

One of Jyl's personal training clients, and the organizer of the Home and Garden Show at the Phoenix Convention Center, presented her with a challenge. If Jyl could get the cookbook finished in three weeks, she would advertise and promote the book for free in newspapers, radio, and at the event. Jyl borrowed $15,000 from her parents to get the book printed. Unbelievably, 1000 copies flew off the tables at the Home and Garden Show in three days. Her book didn't even have a cover yet, but she knew that the public was "hungry" to learn how to cook healthy. People wanted to be educated about a healthier lifestyle, which led to the development of her own publishing company, Family Fit Lifestyles, Inc. Jyl focused on heart-healthy cookbooks created for "busy moms", and her fifth book was picked up by Time Warner Book Group.

Jyl believes that when learned at an early age, health and nutrition will become part of your lifestyle. Returning to her initial career field of education, Jyl began teaching others how to develop a healthy lifestyle (mind, body, and spirit) in the classroom, beginning when her daughter was three years old. She wisely understood that the children would leave school and go home to their parents and share the healthy snacks, activities, and education they learned that day in the classroom. Jyl professes, "Kids do as kids see. They can be very persuasive, and rarely give up until they get whatever it is they want!" As evidence of this, many years after Jyl shared the message with her daughter's third grade class, a young woman approached her in a local supermarket. "Hello, Mrs. Steinback," she said. "I'm Lindsey. I was in Jaime's third grade class. You told me I could do anything, and today, I am that lawyer I told you I wanted to be in third grade!" Jyl shares, "If you can educate and empower one person on a healthier lifestyle and create a difference in their life, it's like a domino effect that goes around the world. I call it "the circle of wellness that works."

Jyl's life was about to take another unexpected turn. "Be careful what you wish for," she exclaims! Holding her first Shape Up US Health and Wellness Expo in Arizona, Jyl sat around a table with a group of community leaders who eventually became Shape Up US' Board of Directors and sponsors. Jyl proclaimed aloud that she wanted to start a nonprofit corporation to pursue her purpose. The next day one of her key sponsors gifted her with an already established nonprofit that he didn't have time to actively run. "Are you kidding me? I just put it out there to the universe saying, 'Okay, universe, what are you thinking about for me?' and this incredible opportunity appeared."

Jyl changed the name of the organization to Shape Up US, Inc., and she was off to the races. She is committed to the Shape Up US mission: to prevent obesity among children, their families, and the entire community. One of their first initiatives, Hip Hop Healthy Heart Program for Children™, is a continuing education program for K-6th grade educators and others who work with elementary-school-age children. The learning flows from teacher to student, student to family members, and on to the community.

Jyl credits her amazing parents with teaching her to envision your success and it will happen. "Just go get it, whatever it is you want to do," Jyl says. She is also inspired by both of her children and welcomes their input. When her seventeen-year-old son told her a Shape Up US Health and Wellness Expo was the best he had ever attended, she knew to pay attention because she had something powerful for youth. She discusses and tweaks Shape Up's various initiatives based on their brilliant ideas and honors their opinions. Her son, in fact, introduced her to Eric James, who partners with Shape Up US in a program called CHOICE, for middle and secondary school-age teens. CHOICE incorporates positive messages about facing peer pressures, decision-making, and the consequences that teens bear for choices they make. Jyl's support emanates from her family and all of her extraordinary friends that made her dreams possible, saying, "They are all an inspiration and guiding light in my life." She climbs the local mountains, a key component of her own physical and mental fitness regimen, to get the endorphins flowing, reinforcing her sense that she can "change the world" and make a huge impact on the health of our Nation. She practices what she professes, feeding herself well, exercising daily, meditating, and surrounding herself with positive people who support her.

When asked about the secret to her success, Jyl is quick to say that no one ever told her she couldn't do it. She says, "It is like going up a mountain with one step in front of the other and just keep on trucking!" She is guided by her spiritual beliefs and staying open and responsive to meeting the right people at the right time. "That's what makes it all come together! The team that has launched this movement is critical to making a huge impact in today's world."

Jyl describes herself as, "extremely persistent and focused, with lots of love to give back. Also, I'm very spiritual, and very tenacious," she says, as she works to garner support for her cause. She says she tries to give back 1000%. "I believe you give back more than you take and you pay it forward. Help someone else with his or her dreams and goals. I believe one 'aha' moment everyday makes it an extraordinary day, and I am totally grateful for each and every one!"

"Yes, I took risks. A lot of them! Every day I took risks. I still am! We are creating Shape Up US Health and Wellness Expo in four states this year and next year with the goal of Shaping Up eight states. We are partnering with remarkable organizations, and I know it's going to happen thanks to everyone who believes in the vision." Her energy and enthusiasm are contagious as she talks about her work. She explains, "It's not work when you love what you do. Everyone should try it. Have a passion and *go for it all!*"

"You have to leave the city of your comfort and go into the wilderness of your intuition. What you'll discover will be wonderful. What you'll discover is yourself."

— Alan Alda

FINDING YOUR NICHE

Have you always known exactly what you wanted to do in your life, or did it take you some time to really figure it out? It seems as if some people easily discover their "it" when they are very young and just go for it. They know what excites them and they plan their career path and life doing something they love. The majority of us, however, do not have a clue and seem to drift from one opportunity to the next, following the path that pays the bills. This job may even provide a terrific lifestyle, but frequently it doesn't feel like it's what we were meant to do.

Looking for clues in our life experiences will help us identify our uniqueness and our passion. Self-discovery is the first step in the process to finding our niche--this place where we can excel.

Gia Heller's Adventures

Gia Heller enters a room and you immediately know that the energy in the room just shifted. She is dynamic. She is also on a mission. Gia charges into life with a passion that is rare to witness and visible to

53

everyone she comes in contact with. Her mother, Meria Heller, says that "Gia ran before she walked and sang before she talked." Gia *always* knew she would be successful and that she would achieve great things in the world. The six women who raised her instilled this belief in her, and their influence shaped her life. As a teen she was bored and she quit high school, got her GED, and enrolled at Phoenix Community College, attending for a semester until she was accepted at Southwestern University in Kansas. She was a gal in a hurry to get on with her life and live her dreams. Gia played Dorothy in *The Wizard of Oz* and other roles, but a career in acting was not to be the next step in her career. She ran her dad's construction company and quickly observed that there was money to be made in real estate. Another door had opened, and she knew she was going to walk through it.

And doors kept right on opening. Next, Donald Trump's show, *The Apprentice*, Season III in 2005, really opened Gia's mind to the reality that she had the ability to create the exact life she craved. Gia attained the twenty-first spot out of 1,000,000 video auditions and went to LA to compete. A strong competitor and confident in herself, Gia made another life-changing decision. Living a unique, dynamic, and diversified life was her priority. She left the corporate world and a six-figure income behind. As a single mother, she moved to Puerto Penasco, Mexico, with her eight- and eleven-year-old daughters. Gia describes the journey "that would prove to be one of the most financially rewarding and emotionally lucrative endeavors I had ever taken on!" Selling more than $20 million in properties in less than three years, she was enormously successful. She, "put her money where her mouth was and invested in real estate, then took the bath of a lifetime." Little did she know then that fate had much grander opportunities in store.

Taking risks is a common thread I discovered in the women I interviewed for this book, and Gia was no exception. "Not taking a job when I got back from Mexico," was a huge risk. I was "humbled, broke, and wondering what the heck it was going to take in this NEW ECONOMY to create abundance again." Gia said, "The greatest single challenge I ever faced was returning from Mexico broke and figuring out what I was going to do."

Gia describes herself as "CRAZY, high energy, aggressive, dynamic and Italian, a native New Yorker, a protective momma bear, and a daughter." These traits, uniquely Gia's, were the basis for discovering her niche and building a new dream. But first, Gia went back to commercial real estate in a market that was spiraling downward at unbelievable speed in Phoenix. Making 125 in-person contacts weekly plus making 125 phone calls weekly resulting in only a "few measly new clients" a month convinced Gia there must be a better way. She began to research using the internet and search engine optimization to get top rankings on Google, knowing this was important. She was seriously intrigued by "the new kid on the block—Social Networking/Media."

During this time Gia's company forced her to form a business leads group. She initially resisted, not seeing the benefit. When her research uncovered the fact that 75% of networkers were women, Gia founded Arizona Women Networking in May of 2009. She also joined Facebook about the same time. Even then she recognized the power of this new tool and the potential benefit it had as a business networking tool. During this early period she was discovering and defining her niche. "The market created the demand, and people were asking me to do this." Her confidence was back after her ego-deflating experience in Rocky Point, and her mother told her, "All you need is a plan!" Gia decided to roll the dice on herself. With her strong desire to succeed, she knew she could do it. Gia's advice to other women is, "Have a plan and persist. Invest in yourself and work smart, not hard." As you travel your own unique path on your individual journey to success, "Do not worry about the opinions of others." She thinks the qualities that make women successful are their aptness to stick to a plan. They are detail oriented, they instinctively build relationships, and they are naturals at referrals. Successful leaders, "listen, determine the needs of those around, and fulfill them. They are authentic and they live a seamless life--they are always the same person. My life and my career are integrated."

Arizona Women Networking expanded to add Arizona Men Networking. Momentum was building and The Phoenix Business Experts was launched, followed by The National Business Experts. Gia's defining moment came when a man purchased the franchise to open The National Business Experts in Minneapolis. "Someone said 'yes' and that took me vibrationally to a new level." The growth and expansion continues with the development of local networking groups within the larger organizations.

Talking to Gia is like taking an adventure trip without a map, not knowing what is around the next curve, even for Gia. I asked her what she wanted her legacy to be and she said, "To turn people's dreams and passions into reality. I want to build a global platform and then reach the children." Then she turned to me and said, "I just got chills! I want to start a nonprofit organization to train children. That just came to me!"

Gia says her 'WHY' is, "I want to win, and I want to bring every-one around me . . . I want to bring them with me!" She's found her niche for today, but ultimately her dream is to help others on a grand scale by becoming a public figure they can trust, learn from her mistakes, and be a role model. Gia wants to *be* the change she wishes to see in the world, and provide others with hope that, *"If she can do it, anyone can."* Gia says, "I want to help hundreds of thousands and even millions of people reach their dreams."

Are you still confused about what you want to be when you grow up? Why not be YOU! Gia's story exemplifies my belief that the journey is not always a straight path, but often meanders in directions that attract us for a time. I believe we have lessons to learn that prepare us for the next opportunity. As we master skills, we recognize new opportunities which prepare us to take the next step along the path in our journey. Learning to integrate our life as Gia does should be our goal.

"And the woman said if I do not stand there will be no shadow to protect my child from the sun"
— *Unknown author*

CHOICES THAT CHANGE US

Some of the choices we face seem monumental, and some are made with barely a thought of the ramifications. But the result of some decisions you thoughtlessly make, can change your life and the life of people around you, forever. Each choice sets us up for the next, and the sum total of those choices brings us to the place we are today.

Christina Wagner's Life-Changing Choice

"We had the perfect life," Christina slowly reflected. "We had a daughter, Skye, who was four and as full of fun and laughter as a child can be, and our infant son, Zephan, who was so loving and happy. My husband and I had a relationship that was playful and fun; we were best friends." He graduated from college and was offered a job in California and, while leaving all her family and friends was a difficult decision, Christina also believed it would be a great adventure and a wonderful opportunity for her husband.

Christina told me the one thing in this world she felt she truly excelled at was being a great mom. She made homemade baby food, and encouraged her children to love art as much as she did, teaching them to paint and make pottery. This was a happy time in her life, and her two children made her complete.

Fast-forward two years after making their move to California, and Christina was working for a fantastic company, getting her first experience in marketing. Her husband's job had evolved, and they now had the opportunity to live anywhere in the country. Christina missed her family and friends, so they made the decision to relocate back to Arizona.

Reveling in the experience of being back among the people she loved and creating a home for her family, Christina had no clue that her world was about to turn upside down. Very soon after returning to Arizona, Christina was faced with learning her husband had done something no wife ever wants to discover, something that had she been a stronger person would have ended their marriage. Christina's husband had been having affairs with other women during their entire marriage. Lacking the strength to leave him, and every day feeling more and more trapped, Christina slowly sank into a world of denial and drugs. Crystal meth became her only friend, the only thing that could numb her pain.

Christina's addiction continued to grow. Her husband lost his job. Without a source of income, her husband resorted to criminal activities, but Christina said, "That is another story and his for the telling, not mine."

Life became an endless cycle of sleeping for days then staying awake for days, of drugs, and of people best left to the alleys of the world. The family and friends she once loved became people to hide from, to lie to, or to simply ignore. The children Christina once cherished became burdens, and finally even they were ignored and left to their own devices.

Child Protective Services came to the house several times, but Christina could somehow pull herself together enough to get them to go away for a while. Finally, as the saying goes, the law would not be denied, and her husband was sent away. Ashamed, yet still an addict, she could only hide out and turn to the criminals around her that were all too eager to take over where her husband had left off. Christina sadly reflected on the insanity of bringing a man into her home, a man who was not her husband, but a boyfriend, and a man who was involved in some very bad activities. She said, "Had I been smart, no had I been sober, I would have sold my house and taken my children with me to my mother's home. But I wasn't sober, so the nightmare continued."

Christina hopes by sharing her story that someone reading this will reach out and ask for help.

"Come out with your hands up! Come out with your hands up!" The sun came up one morning to the sounds of concussion grenades slamming against the house, and the police on bull horns screaming at the occupants of her home. As a dazed Christina came into the hallway, her two shaking children, wearing nothing but pajamas, cried out, "Mommy, is there a war?" Christina remembers saying "No, baby, there's not a war. We just need to go outside." She remembers walking outside to what, in fact, looked like a war zone. The street was lined with police cars and SWAT teams. Her boyfriend was taken into custody, the police took her children away, and then they took Christina in for questioning.

Christina describes the detective as "an angel." He observed the pictures in her home and told her he knew the woman sitting there wasn't who she was. He told her to get sober and no charges would be pressed. Christina and her children went to her mom's, and for a period of time she feigned sobriety. Child Protective Services had gotten involved, and Christina's mother now had guardianship of the children. This was a blow to Christina. One afternoon she wanted to take her children to the park, and her mother told her "no." "I was not taking any recovery classes, and I think I was just looking for a reason to get angry," Christina said, "so I just left."

She went back to her house and her boyfriend and managed to stay sober for three days. Then she fell right back in the same dark life. Her boyfriend's illegal activities expanded to Las Vegas, and she remembers this time-period as "sinking, morally and emotionally, down to new lows. It was a time of becoming totally entrenched in the seedy, ugly, and unsavory aspects of Las Vegas, blowing money on drugs, gambling and shopping, and quickly losing twenty pounds. Life was so intense and so ugly." Christina quietly shares that, "I knew what was going on and I didn't object."

Christina said to me, "You would think that experiencing one raid and losing your children would be enough for you to realize you are in trouble, but I still didn't get it." One afternoon Christina had gone to her mom's to visit her kids and as she was leaving, Christina's mom said to her, "I love you, honey." Christina turned around and said to her, "Why would you love me?" Her mom said, "I don't love the person you're being right now, but I know that somewhere in there is my baby."

As the words her mother spoke to her began to sink in, Christina realized she needed help. She knew that she had to get away from her boyfriend and even from Phoenix. She called her sister in Seattle, who just said "Come!" Christina packed her bag and was about to leave, but her boyfriend refused to let her go. He threw her against the door, put his hands around her neck, and literally lifted her off the ground by the sheer force of his hands on her throat. She said, "At that moment I knew I would never get away from him, and I prayed for the police to come." They did come, but not at that moment.

Operation White Eagle . . . that is what they called the second raid on her house. Twelve homes were raided that day. Christina's picture was on the front page of the newspaper along with twelve other people who were arrested for credit card fraud.

Afterwards, Christina was taken into custody and interrogated. The detectives told her she was going to jail; they began listing potential charges and told her she would not see her children for a very long time. Then they left the room.

With tears streaming down her cheeks, Christina said, "I prayed, 'God, I don't deserve this, but if You can help me, I will put the pieces of my life back together, I will make it right, and I will be the mother that I know I can be.' " "For me" she said, "it was not just a prayer, but a promise." Without warning the detective returned, and his demeanor had completely changed. He said, "I hope you have learned something from this," and he told two other detectives to take her home. "I will never understand what happened; one minute I am going to jail, and the next, I am given another chance."

Christina said, "That moment was the turning point for me." She arrived back to a home that had been ransacked. "I was so grateful to God that he answered my prayers, I will never forget the promise I made; I picked up the phone and called my mother." I cried, "Mom, I've made a wreck of my life, I don't know how to fix it, and I need help."

"Asking my mother for help was the first of many steps in my recovery. I went to every meeting, every group, or counseling session I could find. I was vigilant in my recovery." But it was hard; it was very hard for Christina. Without the numbing drugs, she began to feel the pain of what she had been hiding from, and now she could fully see how she had hurt her children and her family. Christina tried to cope with her emotions using food, and she quickly gained seventy pounds. "In reflection," she said, "I felt ashamed, and I think the weight helped me feel like I was hiding."

Christina was now faced with the task of putting her life back together. An opportunity came from her mother, who started a local advertising company, Darn Good Deals, to promote only locally owned businesses. Christina said, "I wanted to be part of it, and I was excited to do something that would help our local economy." Together, they began attending networking meetings, and they eventually started their own radio show. Christina said, "My mother saw more in me than I saw in myself, and she pushed me to get out in the world. Thankfully, I trusted her enough to take her advice, and it led me to a new path of self-discovery. I began to believe in myself again, to see myself as a healthy, strong, and morally upright person. I found I no longer needed to hide from the world, so I shed the seventy pounds I had gained. I discovered that I loved meeting new people and helping people. I found *my* voice that had been silent for so many years."

Unfortunately, Darn Good Deals did not survive the economic downturn in Phoenix. KFNX Radio had observed the way that Christina networked, handled her clients, and successfully used social media networking. They knew she was a person they wanted on their team, and she was hired as their marketing director.

Currently, Christina is known locally as the AZ Deal Girl, and she recently created the popular "Voice of the Valley" page on Facebook. She will host a new radio show on KFNX beginning in the fall of 2011, and she is on the board of directors for several non-profit organizations. She is a proud member of AZ Women in Media, The National Business Experts, and NAWBO (National Association of Women Business Owners). Christina is a member of the executive board for Rock Me Arizona, and is a Precinct Committeeman for Legislative District 21 for the Republican Party. Christina is passionate about helping local small business owners. She created AZ Social Networking, often known as Christina's 9:05, a dynamic networking event where small business owners can meet and support each other.

"But most, most, most importantly," Christina is excited to share, "my children, my family, and my friends have forgiven me, and allow me the joy and honor of being part of their lives again."

SECTION II

FROM IMPOSSIBLE TO EMPOWERED

"Woman must not accept; she must challenge.
She must not be awed by that which has been built up around her;
she must reverence that woman in her which struggles for expression."
— *Margaret Sanger*

FROM IMPOSSIBLE TO EMPOWERED

As you continue to read the stories and real-life experiences these amazing women courageously shared with you, did you at least once think, "What she did was impossible"? In reality it was not impossible. It was overwhelmingly difficult in some instances, but not impossible. Each journey shaped that person into the individual she is today. Each of these unique women discovered within themselves the ability to look beyond their immediate circumstances and find the self-love necessary to climb out of impossible situations. They knew they were worthy of more, and they were absolutely determined to achieve it. They became empowered through their unique journeys and discovered joy in designing a future of empowered living.

Choose today to believe you can design and experience an empowered and fulfilled life--the one of your heart's desire. Believe in the beauty of *your* dreams. Describe it in detail in the next exercise. It can be yours if you believe.

Discover inspiration and guidance for your personal journey as you continue to share and reflect upon the journeys of other remarkable individuals.

Design Your Dream Future

- How would your life change if you were successful achieving your dreams?

  _____

  _____

  _____

  _____

- What would your job or career be?

  _____

  _____

- Where would you live?

  _____

  _____

- What type of house would you own?

  _____

  _____

- Where would you travel?

  _____

  _____

- What car would you drive?

  _____

  _____

- Would you choose new friends?

  _____

  _____

- What changes would you make in your lifestyle?

  _____

  _____

  _____

- What does your health look like?

  _____

  _____

  _____

- What would you do to give back?

  _____

  _____

  _____

- What does your head say?

  _____

  _____

  _____

- What does your heart say?

  _____

  _____

  _____

- Write down ALL the reasons you are the perfect person to make your dreams a reality.

  _____

  _____

  _____

  _____

  _____

  _____

- Describe, in great detail, the life you want to live. What does your ideal day look like? Be very specific about what your life looks like next year, five years from now and ten years from now.

  My Dream Life:

  _____

  _____

  _____

  _____

  _____

  _____

  _____

  _____

"People who cannot invent and reinvent themselves must be content with borrowed postures, secondhand ideas, fitting in instead of standing out."
— *Warren G Bennis*

REINVENTING YOURSELF

Take a look around at a valuable lesson we can learn from nature and the world surrounding us. Nothing in nature is stagnant. It is constantly evolving, growing, or it is dying. The same is true for each of us. We must constantly grow, learn, and change, or we are going to die as well. This applies to our business, our career, and our life.

LeAnn Hull's Decision to Run for Congress

"I watched my world unravel around me with the events of Wall Street and the economic downturn, and that's when I flew to Washington, D.C., to meet with our congressmen and our senators from Arizona because I wanted them to hear what was happening to *my* business and to *my* life. But I didn't feel like I was heard back there; in fact, I didn't even get to talk to them personally. I only saw their interns. I realized that we, as ordinary citizens, really don't have a voice, so that's what led me into the political arena. It's not like I always had political aspirations; I wanted to be the voice for the ordinary citizen, for contractors, for people like me, small business owners," LeAnn told me as we were discussing her decision to run for Congress in 2010.

This was a very different role for LeAnn, who met her future husband at age fifteen, married at twenty, and had three children by the time she was twenty-five. She loved being a mom, helping at school and being part of the PTA. "I was so young, we grew up together," is how LeAnn describes those early years rearing her family. LeAnn's husband was a teacher. During the summers, they started a remodeling company which became so successful that her husband decided to retire from teaching. When LeAnn and her husband celebrated the unexpected arrival of their fourth child, they reversed their roles. For the next fifteen years, he became a stay-at-home dad caring for their youngest son. During this time he built homes and developed property deals, while LeAnn took over running the construction company. LeAnn had a vision of a company that was diversified in both commercial and residential business to better weather the shifts in the construction industry. She also wanted her business to provide a good living and a good quality of life, which to her meant flexible schedules and keeping her family first.

Married for thirty-one years, LeAnn is passionate about her family. She says that marriage is hard work, and she's proud of the success she and her husband have had, "even though sometimes during those years we didn't like each other very much!"

"For a woman to balance bringing up a family and running a business is very challenging, and it creates a lot of inner turmoil." As LeAnn describes her schedule for the day before, she says she lives hour to hour, moment to moment sometimes. She was a witness in court in the morning, then she did some marketing for a company she was working with, she picked up and delivered windows for a construction job, met with a friend to continue developing their relationship, drove across town to see her son's first varsity game, and then took him to his church youth group meeting. She didn't get home until 9:00 o'clock that evening. But LeAnn made career choices that gave her the ability to be there for her children and she wouldn't have it any other way. Although her life has taken many twists and turns, she tries to not always live for the future, but to make sure she is thriving in the present.

"Success is defined only by you, not by society. If you are doing what everyone else is doing, it is probably not the best choice for you if you want to have your voice heard. It's not that everybody else is wrong. There is a place in society for conformity, but we also need the people that really want to make a mark and be a leader. So if you really are that leader, you have to be okay with your own definition of success. I lost running for Congress. I came in last place. Some would define that as a failure. I define it as a success. I didn't burn my bridges. I didn't destroy my soul in the process, and I am still respected. That's a success," believes LeAnn.

Sharing some of the secrets of her success, LeAnn "starts every day with prayer. I get centered and forgive myself for not always being successful, and every day I start fresh. We have such unrealistic expectations for ourselves as women, as wives, as mothers, as businesswoman, and all of these set us up for failure every day. We are our own biggest enemy. You have to find out what's in you. If you are going to put yourself in a vulnerable position where you are different, then you find out what comes out of you. And I found out. It's not like I knew it or I ever said, 'Wow, I'm going to do this or do that.' It has evolved through my challenges and, little by little, I am discovering my passion. I don't really like being out of my comfort zone, but it's only when I'm out of it that I find out what I'm passionate about and what I'm really good at."

"Running for Congress changed me," she says. "I made a flip decision to do it and people laughed at me. That laughter made me decide even more to do it. I learned who I am on my own, not just as a wife or a mother, but who I really am." LeAnn emphasizes that you must put yourself in different situations to find out what's in you. You have to put yourself out there. Only then do you discover the unique person you are.

As a teen, LeAnn's picture of success was to become a successful attorney or a vice president of a corporation and earn lots of money. LeAnn also had a vision for her children that equaled or excelled the vision she had for herself as a young person. Accepting that when they take a different path, you have to take a step back and ask yourself, "What's this all about?" It was a soul-searching moment for LeAnn, because they had not achieved the level of success she had set for them. I could tell that this was tough for her. Her children were part of her identity, but she learned she had to separate herself from them and allow them the freedom to make their own choices. Today, LeAnn is very proud of two sons currently serving in the military, her daughter who is a nurse, and her youngest son who is an accomplished baseball pitcher and spiritual leader. She knows her influence has taught them the value of serving others.

Challenges are a part of life, and how you deal with them defines you as a person. When LeAnn shifted her identity from being a mother to that of a business woman and the business began to fail, she asked herself, "What do I do, who am I, what value am I, what's my worth?" She began soul searching and found that she was judging herself against other people. Observing someone who had chosen a career path at age thirty and had successfully advanced, compared to her own career path which had gone up and down like a roller coaster, LeAnn had concerns. With her business now failed, she questioned if she was also a failure. "My life has been the e-ticket ride," she exclaims! "When your life doesn't look like the norm, it's difficult enough to deal with. When you are getting input from many others, you have to protect yourself every day and only allow certain information into your life so that you can protect your journey. I think it's important that we be vigilant about protecting ourselves. I am open, but if I'm in an environment that is negative, I will separate myself immediately."

"I don't believe women have to lose their softness in order to be successful," LeAnn shares when discussing the challenges of working in a male-dominated environment, both in business and in politics. "I can still be soft and strong and vulnerable. Dealing with males who want something from me drains my energy. Early in my career, I tried to fit in with the males I worked with. I cussed and dressed more masculine to prove I could fit in and was as tough as they were. But I was denying my femininity and the gift I had been given. I gradually began to change and learned to love who they are and acquire their respect without bruising their egos." LeAnn's passion is impacting lives, and her message to other women is, "Embrace your womanhood! Don't be afraid to try anything. You can be successful and strong and still be sweet . . . that draws people to you. Our womanhood is a gift and don't be afraid of that gift. We are different than men; we should use our special and unique traits, not theirs."

"I figured it out one failure at a time, one closed door, one road-block, one being okay with that, and never being defeated. I've heard people say, 'She's the most passionate person I've met.' The biggest struggle for me is my own self-image. I work on it every day. Maybe that's why God has given me so many challenges. My success with my marriage and my children is because of my attitude."

"My attitude makes me unique. I have a never-quit attitude, and when things are tough, I find someone I can laugh with." LeAnn's zest for life is best understood in her own words, "I love life, being here and experiencing everything I can. I would rather make a mistake than not try. I want to make the most of this life and not miss anything. I want to feel all the emotions I can feel. Only when you've experienced great sorrow can you experience great joy. I don't want to miss anything!"

LeAnn was recently appointed Commissioner with the City of Phoenix Sister City Program, and says, "I have more to do in my life . . . I just don't know what it is yet."

LeAnn continues to reinvent her role in life, but one thing never changes and that is her total passion for the role she is currently living.

"The minute you alter your perception of yourself and your future, both you and your future begin to change."

— *Marilee Zdenek*

GET INPUT FROM PEOPLE WHO KNOW YOU

Let's go back to you and how you can discover what makes you unique. Each of us has blind spots regarding ourselves that make it impossible to see ourselves clearly. These blind spots prevent us from recognizing our positive and negative qualities. We have lived with ourselves so long that we have lost our perspective and ability to step back and see all of the parts that make us who we are. We don't do this intentionally; we just typically don't realize how others perceive us and we seldom ask them. How long has it been since you asked a friend, your family members, or colleagues to give you feedback about yourself? Most of us just are not comfortable doing this. We don't know how reliable their input will be or if they know us well enough to give us input that we can trust. And if we ask, then we must be prepared to do something about their feedback, or why bother asking. So we don't ask.

No other person is exactly like us and that's the exciting news. We are truly unique and special. The challenge then is digging in and discovering how we are unique, and which of our unique skills or traits will contribute to our success.

In the first exercise, you started thinking about your childhood and some of the clues to discovering your uniqueness. In this next exercise, you will be looking closer at your life as an adult. For some of you this may encompass only a few years. For others, you may be looking at a 'lifetime' of experiences as you remember the things that will give you hints to what makes you special.

Remember that no one does it like you do.

Identify Your Uniqueness

- Write down the major successes you have achieved in your life.

_____

_____

_____

- Identify the specific skills you used to attain these successes.

_____

_____

_____

- Describe the emotions you feel as you remember these victories.

_____

_____

_____

- List the skills that seem to come to you naturally and you probably take for granted.

_____

_____

_____

- What qualifies you as an expert in your field?

_____

_____

_____

- Describe the activities that make you truly happy.

  _____

  _____

  _____

- Recall a situation when you found a solution to a problem that no one else could resolve and write it down.

  _____

  _____

  _____

- Think about how you came up with the solution and if this could be a key to a unique ability.

  _____

  _____

  _____

- Describe a time when you came up with a unique idea that was implemented by you or others.

  _____

  _____

  _____

- What unique ability did you use to develop this idea?

  _____

  _____

  _____

- Write down what you would do if nobody paid you to do it.

  _____

  _____

  _____

Ask yourself, "What is my purpose on this planet?" "What is my vision for my future?"

"Champion the right to be yourself; dare to be different and to set your own pattern, live your own life and follow your own star."
— *Wilfred Peterson*

DARE TO BE DIFFERENT . . . BE WHO YOU ARE!

The society we live in encourages us to conform. We rush to purchase the latest fad, be it clothing, electronics, automobiles, or fashion pets. Do you look great in the latest style? Maybe or maybe not, but we buy and wear it because it's the thing to do. We want to fit in. We've been taught to fit in from a very young age and that message is strongly reinforced the moment we enter the traditional education system. Don't rock the boat, color inside the lines, follow the rules, do it this way, and many, many more instructions like this are repeated over and over until we '*get it*'.

But let's remember that each of us is unique and different from any other person on this planet. How terribly boring it would be if we were the same. Many people try so hard to fit in and not stand out. Why?

Yet look at the people we look up to as successful. The business leaders, celebrities, sports figures, great musicians, authors, and artists, and many other roles are successful because of their uniqueness. They excel at the things they do and are unique in what they do.

Whom do you remember when you go to a party, the wallflower or the life of the party? Whom do you gravitate toward at networking events? Is it the person that looks desperate for someone to talk to, or is it the high-energy person that everyone seems to know and wants to talk with? Think about the people you come into contact with on a daily basis whether in person or online. Whom do you spend time with? Why? It is the people who are special. They may be different in any number of ways that attracts others. They have that *something unique* that draws others. People want to become like them. They lead and people follow.

Understanding the personal empowerment that comes with discovering your unique gifts and incorporating them in your personal style is guaranteed to skyrocket you to the next level in your business, your career, and your life.

Nicole Angeline's Journey to Self Discovery

"CRAZY IN HEELS!" A tall, very attractive blonde woman arrived late at a networking event and eyes turned as she walked across the room. Her gorgeous red patent leather stilettoes immediately caught your attention. She was wearing a very unique pendant necklace in the shape of a stiletto with a ruby inset. Her confidence was evident when she introduced herself as Nicole Angeline, and said, "I'm CrAzY in Heels!"

About five years ago, Nicole was sitting at her desk at work feeling enormously frustrated and crying for no reason. She felt like throwing every object in sight; her emotions were on a roller coaster and spiraling downward. Recognizing that something was wrong with her and seeking professional help, she first heard the words, "I think you are bipolar." Nicole's reaction was "Thank God, I finally know what is wrong! Can I have some medication so I can get better?" Her attitude has always been, "If something is wrong, fix it!" Just putting a name on her condition set Nicole on a path of researching and learning everything she could about Bipolar II Disorder. She says, "Apparently, I am a far cry from what society deems as normal. So, with that being said . . . I say 'bring it on! Being bipolar doesn't make me crazy; it makes me CrAzY in Heels!' "

Looking back now, Nicole says, "I could see the symptoms starting from the time I was about fifteen years old." Her early years were not always easy. As a child Nicole and her mother felt as though there was something wrong, as Nicole had a hard time sitting still and focusing in class, and while doing homework. She was tested for Attention Deficit Hyperactivity Disorder (ADHD), but it wasn't until in her early twenties that the actual medical diagnosis was made. Her mother, whom she describes as amazing, had been through a couple of divorces, and they left Nicole's dad behind when they moved to Arizona. Nicole admires and loves her mother, and she now recognizes the difficulties her mother faced as a single parent bringing up a child with ADHD. For Nicole, her condition translated into stress at school, where she was not doing well and was frequently getting poor or failing grades. She began believing all of the negative self-talk that started filling her head, "I'm pretty, I'm stupid; I'm blonde, I'm stupid; no one takes me seriously!" Her mother felt that something was wrong, but everyone kept telling her that Nicole was fine. Nicole recalls that during her high school years she would "sometimes stay up all night, talk on the phone, feel really 'up' and overinflated with confidence, but then I would crash."

"I probably have enough credits to have a college degree, but I don't have one," Nicole shared. "I went to five different colleges." By the time she went off to her third college, Nicole had turned to drugs to self-medicate. She started working as a VIP hostess at one of the big clubs in Scottsdale, and was constantly surrounded by opportunities to access 'party drugs'. "I had some pretty wild and crazy times" she acknowledged. Finally, with her weight dropping to ninety pounds and knowing she had a problem, Nicole reached out for help. She went through an outpatient rehabilitation program, left the clubs and temptations behind, and went to work as a receptionist.

Nicole worked as a receptionist for an insurance agent of one of the countries well-known mutual insurance companies for over five years. Because she didn't have a college degree, her self-confidence was low. She continued to believe she was a "dumb blonde" who could do no more with her life than sit at the front desk, because that is what every man who hired her wanted her to do. "I'm fully licensed in Arizona to sell property, life, casualty, and health insurance. That's not easy to do!" Nicole demonstrates her new beliefs about herself, leaving behind the old constraints of believing she was stupid. Deciding it was time to make some changes, Nicole left the insurance company and went to work for an independent broker. At the same time she returned to school, this time with a 4.0 grade point average, all while planning a wedding and starting a new job. "I'm not that 'pretty' girl that needs to sit at the front desk anymore! I can do anything I want to do, and I'm going to go do it," her eyes shining with excitement as she shares these words.

A year before she left the insurance office Nicole went on a trip to California with her husband, Brian. She describes him as "driven, highly motivated, and he had all these friends and graduated at the top of his class at Arizona State University. I compared myself to him . . . he didn't, but I did." They were driving and Brian made Nicole listen to a

Millionaire Mind motivational CD. Her first thoughts were, "This man is crazy; I can't believe I'm marrying him. But then I started really listening to the CD's. That last year I was at the insurance company, I listened to them every single morning, and I never missed a morning. "Millionaire Mind," "Happy for No Reason," "The Secret" . . . I learned more from listening to those motivational CD's than I ever learned in college. Without a doubt, the power of affirmations is the key to what changed my life. When I heard T. Harv Eker talking about the power of the subconscious mind and learning to change your thoughts, I began saying affirmations every day, and now they just play in my head. I tell people to just start saying their own affirmations once a day, then twice a day, and keep saying them."

After a year of repeating her affirmations, Nicole had the confidence to begin making changes in her life. Accepting another front desk position because it was the only thing the firm had at the time, she was excited because they were going to give her the opportunity to become an agent. Nicole started attending networking events and loved meeting and talking with people. Soon she was invited to become president of Power Networking, a large networking group.

"I wish people could see how my life has changed!" Nicole is very emotional as she describes feeling so tiny and insignificant only a year earlier. "I'm not that dumb blonde girl sitting at the front desk any longer! People take me seriously now and I want others to know they can do what I did," Nicole is crying as she shares her happiness at finding her passion and the confidence and belief in herself to fulfill her dream. I am also crying with her, as I listen to this beautiful person recall the darkness and the journey to her discovery of self and all she has become today.

"Before learning I was bipolar, no one young and fun was telling me what was wrong with me," Nicole shared. "All of my information was coming from books written by older, stuffy doctors with PhD's and nothing I could relate to. So much of what I read was negative and dark and, when you are going through something like this, you want to see the light at the end of the tunnel!" I had all this research I wanted to share with people, so they wouldn't have to go through what I did. I told my brother, who did web design, about my idea to start a website as a resource. My goal was to have it be uplifting, positive, bubbly and just me! I was in bed one night when it just came to me . . . CrAzY in Heels! It was just right because I am always in heels, even at the grocery store, and my husband tells me I'm crazy." She launched CrAzY in Heels, LLC, and got her website up and running. She was then asked to become president of a second networking group. Due to the success of CrAzY in Heels, Nicole now juggles the duties of running her own business, starting the "CrAzY and Loving It" non-profit charity, and raising awareness within her local community.

"I want to erase the stigma of unstable, emotional, scattered, or bizarre behavior! So many people just take it too seriously," Nicole explained. "I'm crazy, so just take it or leave it! I am going to create a better awareness of bipolar disorder so people will think: 'successful, creative, imaginative, and caring'." She began using social media to promote her website, and the word spread rapidly. Visitors to her website started posting very upbeat comments about her positive approach to living with bipolar disorder. She blogs and provides many resources for people with bipolar disorder along with information and resources for their families. Nicole also speaks to young people in the schools to raise awareness of the condition and help them understand how you can take charge and control your life. She tells young women to "work on '*you*' and get in touch with who you really are and what you really think. You must block out all of the negative input from outside and work on developing your inner self."

"If you are not doing something you love in your life that you *really* love, find it! That's where the person you really are starts to come out. Anything is possible if you just take the steps; I am proof of that," she excitedly says.

Nicole is stepping into her future with confidence and she is having a great time . . . She's *CrAzY In Heels* . . . gorgeous red ones!

"Don't Let the Fear of Striking Out Keep You From Playing the Game."
— *Babe Ruth*

GET OUT OF YOUR COMFORT ZONE

Are you limiting your success and your personal and career development by continuing to do the same things you have always done? Your life will not change unless you take action. Pushing back your personal boundaries and expanding your comfort zone is essential to achieving your dream life.

Children have no boundaries when they come into this world. They learn to walk, run, climb, explore, and experiment. Adults teach them boundaries. Listen to what people say to their children: "Don't", "you can't", "that's silly", "you'll hurt yourself", "that's stupid," and so much more!

As a child, you believe what others tell you and those beliefs shape your life. You develop boundaries and comfort zones based on those beliefs, and then you act within the boundaries of your comfort zone. You traveled to where you currently are in your life based on those beliefs and boundaries. You aren't even aware many of them exist.

Do you fear making presentations or suggestions in company meetings or at organizations you belong to? Is it possible everyone laughed at something you said during "show and tell" in kindergarten and you were embarrassed? Since you did not have the skills to understand why they were laughing, you accepted a belief about your ability. Are you still living with this belief today and fear speaking in group situations? I challenge you to shatter this false belief and accept that people value what you say!

Examples abound of beliefs we accepted without ever challenging the source. The fantastic news is that we don't have to let those beliefs continue to hold us back. We can identify those false beliefs and get rid of them. You must do this to succeed in pursuing your goals and your dreams!

Kassey Frazier Creates Her Future

"Don't be scared, you have to trust in yourself," is Kassey's advice to other teens beginning their personal and unique journey on the path of life. Confident and enthusiastic, Kassey describes her life as exciting and exactly what she wants to be doing. She attends Horizon High School in Phoenix, and is taking online classes to accommodate her schedule to make time for her TV and radio shows and her many volunteer activities. "Pink is my favorite color and my pink bedroom is SO 'princess.' I love Skittles and could eat a whole bag at one time; and I LOVE cats, but have a dog named Ginger that I am totally responsible for." Kassey shared that "my most prized possession is a ruby ring, my birthstone, and a gift from my grandmother before she passed away. She was the only person who gave me rubies and it was something special we shared," smiled Kassey as she remembers the grandmother who always told her she could do whatever she decided she wanted to do.

Rewind Kassey's life story five years and her life was on a very different path. At age ten, Kassey's mother Liz tells about a teacher who discussed Kassey's shyness and made a recommendation that Liz find a way to help Kassey overcome it. Liz began her quest to help her daughter and discovered an organization that literally changed Kassey forever. National American Miss was a pageant system that Liz thought would help Kassey gain self-confidence and develop stronger communication skills, and convinced her to enter the pageant. "I was terrible and so scared I was shaking," Kassey describes her first pageant, "but my family told me I was great!" "No one is perfect the first time they do anything. You have to keep practicing. My mom would trick me when I didn't want to practice by asking me to tell her about my platform or discuss an issue!" Kassey admits doing the first pageant because her mother wanted her to, but she exclaimed, "Are you kidding?" when Liz suggested not doing the next one. Kassey was having fun and was ready to go for the crown. She won her first crown at age thirteen and recognized the value she was gaining from her experiences. In seventh grade her class was assigned a book report where they were also required to 'dress to impress' for their presentation. She wore a suit and, using her newly acquired presentation skills, received an 'A+' on her report.

Kassey knows she is not a typical fifteen-year-old teen, and her vision is to be a role model for the next generation. "It scares me that the next generation is going to be running the country. The examples set by the celebrities in Hollywood and the athletes whose lives are falling apart show a desperate need for role models the next generation can look up to and learn from. I want to show them that you don't have to 'wait until you grow up'; you can live your dream now."

Kassey's resume states her ambition is to attend the Walter Cronkite School of Journalism and become a TV spokesperson and radio personality. She currently hosts her own radio show on Voice America

Kids, and she interviews other role models who are making a positive difference in the world. She excitedly shared the news that Alice Cooper has agreed to be interviewed on her show. *Runway Role Models*, the second-highest ranked program on Voice America, has an international audience and is now available on Itunes. She just received an opportunity to host her own TV show on Voice America, called *"Kassey Frazier: Behind the Biz."* Kassey plays the lead role in an independent film titled, *Mage*, produced by KidStuff Films, and she will be appearing in another movie, which will begin filming in the summer of 2011. Kassey will be the youngest editor-in-chief in the nation with the September launch of her fashion magazine, *Bella Vita Moda*, and she was asked by Brittany Brannon, Miss USA Arizona, to interview guests at her send-off party at Donald Trump's Miss USA Pageant in Las Vegas. She recently signed with Ranalli Models and is being considered for a positive reality TV show about her BUSY life.

Kassey juggles school and homework with her career and projects she is passionate about. She is the spokes model for "Project Radiant", and volunteers with Teens Caring for a Cause, an organization that recently hosted "The Tiara Tea Party for Make-A-Wish Foundation. She started a nonprofit organization, "Girls Just Want to Have Fun", volunteered in the Fountain Hills Thanksgiving Day Parade to benefit Holiday Mail for Heroes, and had fun as a runway model for "Catwalk for a Cause" which benefits the American Cancer Society and Luv Shack Ranch Horse Rescue. Kassey volunteers at her church and helped an organization called Stop Hunger Now package 10,000 meals that will be sent to Haiti to help school children there.

When I asked Kassey how she is perceived at school, she was quick to say that she doesn't tell others at school about her life away from school. Her experience in seventh grade at a different school was, 'the worst', when crying to her mother, she questioned how to deal with her friends reactions to what she was doing. She quickly decided that she had to focus on her education and what she wanted from life. She looked to her mom and her grandmother for the advice she needed and acknowledges how fortunate she is. "We take for granted what we have, and I realize others don't always have moms they can turn to."

Discussing the pageant, I asked Kassey how she selected her platform and her reply was, "It was chosen for me . . . I have five siblings who look up to me. It's my job to be a role model for them." Her platform and passion is, "Take the Lead! Being a Leader and Role Model in Today's Society." Her family is the hub and support in her life, yet Kassey's vision stretches far beyond her family. "I want people to say that '*because of Kassey Frazier, I am who I now am, and that's who I want to be!*' "

The legacy Kassey envisions is serving her country, the United States, through countless volunteer efforts to improve the quality of life for others. She strives to be a positive influence so others will also become role models and make differences in someone else's life. She seeks to create personal connections with every person she encounters and to let them know they are important, they are making a difference, and someone they might not even know, looks up to them.

As I was interviewing Kassey, I thought to myself how inspiring it was listening to her. At fifteen, she has gained wisdom many people don't acquire over a lifetime. She stepped out of her comfort zone to learn lessons she knows are important to the career and life she wants to experience. "So many people give up . . . don't give up! Do it again and learn from your mistakes. My grandmother always challenged me saying, 'Why not? Take the stepping stones that lie ahead of you or sink in the mud!' "

Success means different things to everyone. For some teens, it is getting great grades leading to a good college and career. For others, it may be winning an athletic event or tournament. For Kassey, success means striving to be who she wants to be. She emphasizes that always staying positive is key. "Who takes this job more seriously than me!" she proudly exclaims as she tells me that she won both Miss Congeniality and Miss Teen in the America's National Teen Pageant when she was fifteen. It was important to her to get to know the other girls in the pageant and not try to diminish any other person.

Kassey didn't always believe she would be successful. She was scared and didn't know if she could do it or if it would work, but she took her grandmother's advice to always go for it. Today, Kassey advises others "to stay strong and stay true to yourself. It's sometimes easier to give up, but complete one thing and go on to the next. I think you can do anything you want to do!"

A "Law of Attraction Board" is on the wall in Kassey's bedroom, and two words on this board are inherent to Kassey's identity. The words "strength" and "love" are there because she wants them to always be part of her.

Kassey shares that people often want to know personal facts about her, and she loves Facebook as a tool to do this as well as a way to get out there what she wants to say. She loves collecting Marilyn Monroe memorabilia, and loves having played Kinect with Danica Patrick. She knows she is unique and has a great sense of style. She is a bargain shopper, frequently finding treasures at consignment stores and Goodwill.

She says, "I am fifteen and doing all these great things!"

I say keep your eyes on Kassey . . . she *will* be a role model for the next generation.

"Age may wrinkle the face, but lack of enthusiasm wrinkles the soul."
— *Danish Proverb*

AGE IS NOT AN EXCUSE

Look around you at the people you see each day. Some people believe they are too old to learn something new or start a new project and seem to have lost their zest for living. Each day becomes routine, and the excitement of new challenges has vanished. The spring in their step is gone, and they carry an air of sadness about them. I was talking to my neighbor recently, and he was excited about still being able to sing in the choir at his church and stand during the entire service. He's ninety-three! I once sent my elderly father an old computer . . . his first . . . He initially rejected the idea, thought about it for a while, and then with no directions, he put it together and began using it. He had an insatiable curiosity about how things worked. Age is not a barrier . . . unless you let it become one.

Joan Spalding's Interview with Eleanor Roosevelt, and Meeting with Mikhail Gorbachev

At age seventy-three, Joan exclaims, "I have so much more to learn, I am going to need another fifty years!" This emotional statement comes from a woman who has experienced amazing adventures in her life and has plans for many more!

"I can see your future now! You are going to marry Art George. He lives up on the hill in that tin shack and he doesn't have any teeth." Joan's father told her. "I knew he was joking, but I told him, 'Just watch me!' I was going to get an education because living in a tin shack wasn't going to be my future." Joan's dad, with an eighth-grade education, and her mother, with less education than her dad, were rearing their family in Wisconsin. Knowing Joan's interest in occupational therapy, her father took her to a mental institution to spend a day to see if caring for people was what she really wanted to do. Somehow, despite caring for ten children, he found a way to raise $100, and she got a scholarship for another $100 and started college. The oldest of ten siblings, Joan, who describes herself as a farm girl, was the first of her family to attend college, investing her total focus into the experience.

"Eleanor Roosevelt slowly walked into the room and I was struck immediately by her humility. She was so interested in asking questions of this crazy group of college women from Wisconsin State University. We were there for an International Relations Conference as representatives of that department at the school. I thought, 'here is a woman who has done so much for the world, and she is sitting here, so gracious and so humble, talking to us and answering our questions.' It taught me a valuable lesson about humility."

Joan's adventurous spirit led her to Yellowstone National Park in 1957, after she noticed a tiny sign at the school advertising a need for summer workers at the park. Everyone thought she was crazy to go, but Joan and a friend got on a train and headed to Yellowstone for the summer to earn money for school, and indulge in her lifelong love of being in the outdoors. Little did she know, this decision would result in her meeting the man who would eventually become her husband and lifelong partner in adventure. Mike Spalding drove from Arizona to Yellowstone in a car that couldn't go any further without repairs. He had five dollars in his pocket and was a week short of his eighteenth birthday. Joan laughingly tells how her first test for Mike as a boyfriend was, "whether he could fish," so she took him fishing. "He really wasn't much of a fisherman," Joan remarked. He did pass the test, and they married three years later, eventually settling in the gorgeous foothills of the Rocky Mountains in Colorado.

Skiing down a beautiful slope at Winter Park Ski Resort in Colorado is an awesome experience. Imagine doing it blind! "All of your senses go immediately to your feet," is how Joan described it. "I had to ski blindfolded as part of my training to teach and guide blind skiers. My initial motive wasn't entirely altruistic; I could get free ski passes for my entire family." By this time Joan and Mike had six children and she wanted them to experience the outdoors. Joan tells of meeting Lloyd Bridges as he got off the ski lift. He was at a celebrity fundraiser for the handicapped skier program and Joan had been asked to interview him for the brochure, magazine, and several newspaper articles. "I watched him get off the lift, and I was just amazed how bowlegged he was!" He said, "Come on, Joan, let's get to it." "We sat down, he propped his feet up and we talked about many things," Joan related, and I thought about the little farm girl from Northern Wisconsin who had just met and interviewed another celebrity.

I recall another exciting ski-related episode soon after I met Joan. She dropped my husband and me off at Winter Park so we could downhill ski and then took off by herself to cross country ski. Looking up, she saw a huge bull moose in her path. "We just stood there without moving and watched each other for over a half hour," she said. It was potentially a very dangerous situation for Joan, but unfazed by this event, she returned to pick us up and shared this amazing experience.

"Mike and I are kind of big picture people and we're not really good on the details . . . you know that about me," Joan said. "We had this dream of building this home ourselves and we had no idea of how much time, how much effort, or how much money it was going to take." Joan and Mike built one of the first solar-powered homes in Colorado. They built it themselves and it took eight years. The challenges were huge and they had much to learn. The base part of their home, which is situated in a beautiful meadow in the foothills of the Rocky Mountains in Colorado, was initially built of a patchwork of plywood that had been thrown away by home contractors in the area. Joan lived in this area of the house for five years with her husband and six children. She went to school to learn to be a carpenter to build her house. It took two years for the school to admit her, and they only did so when she suggested she would really push the issue publicly.

The University of Colorado helped them with the mechanics of the solar system, now thirty-five years old and still operational. The children helped Joan and Mike put nineteen ton of rock on a conveyor belt to move it into the room where it would be heated. They used glass patio doors for the panels, and the first time it got so hot it melted the caulking. The second attempt resulted in the caulking between the glass melting, and they had to cut out part of the glass and change the design. Joan laughingly recalls sitting on a stump in the yard and saying, "what have we gotten ourselves into?" after the second failure, but realized they just had more to learn. She never considered quitting.

After the house was built and the children grown, Mike announced to Joan, "we're going to Russia! That's where we are needed, and it's time to give back." So began the quest to teach others and learn over a total of nine or ten trips to Russia. It was also the beginning of her discovery of a passion for the people of this country who became her friends and taught her much about their lives and their spirit. Joan smiled as she talked about Mike's vision and their challenge of raising the funds for this journey. "Mike wrote to Tom Clancy, the well-known author, telling him about their goals. He called us and wished us well, but he didn't give us any money." You can't be afraid to ask . . . you never know where you will find your support. They packed their belongings, rented their house, and began their first adventure to Russia. Joan taught at Russia's Open University and began building relationships and trust with the people in a country who believed you had to "eat a pound of salt" before you could be trusted. "That meant you had to spend a lot of time eating together and talking before a trusting relationship was achieved."

Mike had returned home in 1992, but Joan stayed on to develop a summer program for the university. Professor Bim-Bad noticed Joan missed Mike and asked her to attend a major World Peace Conference. "Somehow, I was allowed to interview Mikhail Gorbachev," Joan states. Mikhail Gorbachev told me, "Joan, you think the policies of Russia are made in meetings like this one, but the policies of Russia are made in the kitchens of Russia." Joan tells me she didn't know what he meant then, but when she returned to the university, Professor Bim-Bad asked me what Mikhail Gorbachev had talked about. Joan explained her confusion with his statement, and the professor told her he didn't know that Mr. Gorbachev even knew that the policies were made in the kitchens. He told Joan that if water was running, the bugging devices could not record what was being said for spies to hear. "The Russian people survived because of the tremendous networks that were created and the trust resulting from these networks."

"Because of the shortages that occurred during the early 1990s, we had to stand in long lines to get food . . . bread, and it was unbelievable to find eggs." Joan returned numerous times to Russia, witnessing many changes and developing strong friendships. Once while there, she was assaulted at knifepoint and robbed. Her feisty personality had her chasing her assailants yelling, "Thief, thief," but no one understood English. A Russian friend once told Joan that even though she wore Russian clothes and spoke Russian, she would never be mistaken for a Russian because, "You have the look of freedom in your eyes."

Joan passed along her sense of adventure to her children. Once when her son, Steve, was climbing Mount McKinley in Alaska, Joan and another son, Mike, decided to hike the Chilkoot Trail and meet Steve when he came off the mountain. So, packing a thirty-five pound pack on her small frame, she headed up a trail that had left sixty miners dead from an avalanche during the Alaskan Gold Rush.

Joan's determination to learn more about her family took her to Croatia recently, where she found many old records in a village church which led her to meet many of her family members. With the help of translators, she was able to enjoy sharing much information with them. From there, she traveled on to Medjugorje, Bosnia-Herzegovina to visit the shrine where the Virgin Mary is said to appear. This spiritual experience fulfilled one of Joan's dreams. Joan has a strong faith and draws peace and power from this faith. She describes her son, Steve, as one of her spiritual teachers. His death when he was hit by a vehicle while riding his bicycle was devastating. She remembers when he was a senior in high school; he told her he was going to hitchhike to Alaska. "I had to let him follow his own path," Joan said.

Amidst all of her adventures Joan continued her education, studying the effects of educational kinesiology and neuro-reflex integration in the classrooms of Russia and the United States. At age sixty-eight she proudly received her Ph.D. from Colorado State University. She applied her research to the curriculum she developed for an after-school program for students with learning challenges. This program has been approved by the Colorado State Education Department and is taught in many schools. She also maintains an office where she works with young people and adults who want to improve their ability to learn.

Joan describes her achievements and her adventures as "opportunities for living." Her determination and tenaciousness led her to teach classes in Belize while on a vacation where she was learning to scuba dive. She was about sixty-five at the time. She accompanied my husband and me to Mexico where we touched the whales that swam up to our small boats. I remember helping pull her out of the rapids once on a white water rafting trip in southern Colorado. Thirty-five years ago she wrote an article for the paper, saying "throw away your dish cloths, hide your dirty pans, and meet me with your backpacks and skis . . ." Fifteen women showed up and Mountain Mamas was formed. Together they have skied, biked in Switzerland, hiked the Grand Canyon, and still gather today to celebrate their friendship.

"People call me 'The Tree Lady of Evergreen'," Joan shares as she tells me about starting a business selling and relocating large trees, which she still owns. She radiates energy as she tells me about conducting a workshop in a senior center where she teaches older people techniques for better balance. Just last year she had both knees replaced at the same time so she would only have to complete rehab once!

She advises people to really know what you want, picture the end result, and ask yourself if you are still going to want it in five years. Follow your dreams and keep looking for new ones. Just imagine where they might take you. Just imagine a lifetime of adventure!

"Nothing is impossible; there are ways that lead to everything, and if we had sufficient will, we should always have sufficient means. It is often merely for an excuse that we say things are impossible."
— *Francois De La Rochefoucauld*

THERE ARE NO EXCUSES

It's so easy to place blame on others for what happens to us or to say everything that happens is "bad luck." Circumstances are not always our fault, but how we respond to those circumstances will determine the course of our lives. When we are born into difficult situations, it would be easy to believe we are simply victims who can do nothing to improve our life. Life is what you make it and nothing can stop you but you.

CiCi Berardi Accomplished the Impossible

Cici Berardi is a successful business owner and creator of "Fess Up Reality Show," a bold, new program showcasing the "Movers and Shakers" in Arizona. She goes behind the scenes to spotlight "Who Really is Who" in business, entertainment, politics, and sports and persuades these extraordinary people to "Fess Up" about themselves in a positive, insightful, and sometimes funny way. She interviews the frequently familiar faces of innovative leaders in the community with confidence and skill, eliciting the inside scoop that her audience doesn't know about them.

She has a fifth grade education!

"Not having a mother who loved you was the worst," said Crucita Ann Stevens Berardi, who grew up in Philadelphia. Born to unwed parents, she lived with her grandparents, not understanding why her mother came to see her, but had, in reality, abandoned her. CiCi, who is African American, shared that her grandfather was a "white guy" so she grew up in a better neighborhood, never knowing about the ghetto or the "projects." This seven-bedroom house was occupied by twenty-seven people that included her grandparents, cousins, and an aunt who was only four years older than she. CiCi recalls being locked up in the basement, afraid of the "boogey man" and living much of her early life in fear. She learned about racism in her own home, where the members were "all different colors"; the darker ones had to sit at a different table than the ones with lighter skin. Her grandparents claimed to be very religious people, but lived a double standard, not practicing what they professed to believe. CiCi and her younger sister knew some of the events happening in their lives couldn't be 'right', but they were too young to understand and could only try to protect each other. She remembers learning to 'dream' when bad things happened to her and realized she had to be strong to survive.

CiCi was an excellent student, but she wasn't allowed to go to school after fifth grade because the school nurses would have seen the marks of physical abuse on her and reported it to the authorities.

CiCi ran away when she was only thirteen, after learning of her grandmother's death. She was placed in a foster home and was now in the system. When CiCi was fourteen, her mother "showed up out of the blue" and took her, her brother, and her sister to live with her in a home in one of the projects. Her mother could only qualify for the housing if she had her children with her. CiCi lived here for about six months, experiencing many beatings at the hand of her mother's boyfriend. After being held hostage, she and her siblings finally escaped this situation when a neighbor called the police. Her mother's boyfriend shot and killed two policemen and was finally shot himself right in front of CiCi. CiCi said that for many years after this incident she kept waking up screaming and 'seeing' blood all over her.

When CiCi was fifteen, she discovered she had a gift that would free her from being under any other person's control. She started braiding hair for $20 and earned the money that would provide her means to escape. CiCi slept at the police station every night. One day this "church guy", who was actually a police corporal, asked her if she had a place to stay. The church guy and his wife offered CiCi a room for $100 a week, but after her past experiences, CiCi wanted nothing to do with staying in anyone's home. Even though this older couple really wanted to help her, CiCi had had no life experience that would allow her to trust others. She continued to braid hair and was soon able to rent space and open her own shop at sixteen years of age. Soon after this she rented her own apartment and later upgraded to a nicer place, and she was proud of being able to take care of herself.

One day CiCi was sitting in a club with friends when a "white guy" started talking to her, asking her if she ever traveled anywhere. He eventually asked her if she knew how to get to the airport. She claims "I was so naïve, but I told him and his friends to follow me. I wasn't getting in their car, but I drove an hour to the airport with them following me." I was twenty-nine at the time. The guy sent me a ticket to come to Arizona. "I'm this cute girl who can't talk well and he told me I was stupid, but I went," CiCi said. "When I got to Arizona, he sat me down and showed me his checkbook and told me that if I would stay in Arizona, go to school and watch his house, he would give me $15,000 a month."

"He brought me here as an experiment and he had no expectations of me. He was a wealthy corporate executive who was bored and wanted to do something good. He enrolled me in a community college, but I skipped going to school because I didn't have enough education to keep up. I didn't realize at the time how controlling he was, and I wasn't used to having someone telling me what to do and how to do it. He wanted me to go to school and do something with my life, but I already had a life. He never asked me what I wanted," CiCi shared. "If someone told me to do something in those days, I did the opposite!" She stayed for four years, but finally told him she had to do it on her own and left.

CiCi needed her independence, not anyone telling her what to do, and she needed to earn a living. Someone suggested topless dancing and she began working at an exclusive gentlemen's club in Phoenix. She was earning $250,000 a year and spending her money on the things she wanted in her life. She said, "I was the only black chick there and men were paying a lot of money to see me take off my top!" Two years later she walked out of the club saying, "this is not who I am!" She had the lifestyle she wanted, but not the future she envisioned for herself. The little girl who always fought for survival had an unbelievable desire to make something of her life. She never heard the words "I love you" as a child, but her little sister always told her she was special. CiCi believed her and despite all the things that could have destroyed her, she loved herself enough to keep striving for something better.

With some money in the bank, CiCi decided she wanted start her own business, so she began to hostess at high end restaurants. "Everyone was hiring me," CiCi exclaimed. But the reality of dealing with people who were very demanding and often not very nice was an experience CiCi didn't want to continue. Taking stock of her assets, she decided her Hummer would be a great vehicle to transport people around the area. She got her chauffer's license and an advertisement in the Yellow Pages and was in business, taking people to the airport and chauffering proms. CiCi quickly realized that there was only one of her and only so much she could do.

About this time CiCi met Randy. Self-employed, he was selling windows and doors, and CiCi decided she could help him market his business. Although she didn't realize it at the time, she had acquired a significant business education from the man who brought her to Arizona. Looking to the future, CiCi started You Go Boy Marketing and Website, Inc., which is one of the businesses she runs today. After twenty-four years, Randy was getting tired of the window and door business and decided to close his business. CiCi recognized the financial potential in Randy's business and since the phone kept ringing, she went to the Arizona Corporation Commission and registered Enterprises Windows and Doors by Colleen and went to work.

"I was shaking and so scared!" That's how CiCi described her decision to marry Randy last year. They had been together six years and even though Randy kept proposing, CiCi had been so independent for so long and had memories of her early years that made it hard for her to commit to a marriage. She finally said "yes" and they are now happily married and working in the window and door business together. CiCi is passionate about helping young people and has volunteered with Big

Brothers Big Sisters since 2005. She brings some of her young relatives to stay with her and hires them in her businesses to help them get through difficult times in their own life. CiCi will help anyone who needs help, if they have the drive and motivation to make something of themselves.

Armed with a fifth grade education and a strong will to succeed, CiCi taught herself everything she's learned to build four businesses and live the life she wants. She had no one to guide her and learned most of her lessons by trial and error. Today she carries a recorder with her and practices speaking and critiquing herself, so she will continue to improve her skill. CiCi has a quiet pride in what she has accomplished. She truly believes there are people out there, "willing to help you if you are willing to help yourself."

During the darkest of times, CiCi never gave up hope, and today she smiles often.

"Life is a gift, and it offers us the privilege, opportunity, and responsibility to give something back by becoming more."
— *Anthony Robbins*

ACCEPTING PERSONAL RESPONSIBILITY

It's easy to say, "It's not my fault! Life isn't fair!" And maybe life isn't always fair and your parents weren't wealthy enough to pay for your college education, you were too short to get a basketball scholarship, your boss doesn't like you, or . . . or . . . and the list could keep going on. The reality is that you did have choices. Maybe not as an infant, but at a very young age you learned that your actions and choices had repercussions. What happened when you threw a tantrum when you were two years old? And as you continued to mature, your actions and choices resulted in the person you became. If your parents didn't have the resources to pay for your college education, you had decisions to make. If you truly wanted a college education, you could have chosen to excel in your studies or athletics to qualify for scholarships or other forms of financial aid. That choice was yours and is what accepting personal responsibility is all about. It means that you understand that you, alone, are responsible for your life choices and must accept the results of those choices.

Marsha Petrie Sue Took Charge of Her Destiny

"People need to hear the message of personal responsibility!" Marsha dares people to take personal responsibility for their choices, successes, and life. "She has been described as the Muhammad Ali of personal development, leadership, communications, and managing change. She can dance and look pretty and she uses the entire ring, but she knows how and when to land a knockout punch," said David Rawles of Career Solutions. A best-selling author and professional speaker, Marsha is as comfortable at black tie affairs as she is camping in the dirt! Her mission is to give back more than she receives, and to help people see themselves in a better light. Marsha defines success as "what energizes you and makes you feel whole . . . children, career, volunteering . . . whatever brings you joy." She says one of the secrets of her success was "not taking myself too seriously!" She recommends finding balance and not letting any one thing stress you out or trying to be the perfect person in every aspect of your life. "Wear your underwear inside out! Remember how your mother told you to always wear clean underwear in case you were in an accident? Well, just wear them inside out and you will always know you are not perfect," she says. "Only God is perfect."

Breaking through glass ceilings in the corporate world gave Marsha insight and skills that she shares in bestselling books, *Toxic People: Decontaminate Difficult People at Work Without Using Weapons or Duct Tape* and also *The Reactor Factor: How to Handle Difficult Work Situations Without Going Nuclear*. She never says, "I can't, only I choose to or I choose not to do something."

Marsha's first job after graduating college was as a kindergarten teacher, but she disliked every moment of it. She chose at age twenty not to have children, so being a kindergarten teacher was not the smartest choice she ever made in her life, admits Marsha. "Would you like to be a 'candy girl?' " was the ad that caught her eye when she looked for a job doing *anything* but teaching. She decided to take the plunge and began working for a chocolate manufacturer in a low income part of Los Angeles, transporting her melting chocolate samples in an old VW without air conditioning. Marsha's message is "to take risks", and emphasizes how important that is for women to learn because "we've been told not to, we can't, or we shouldn't because we're girls. And that's partly where the glass ceiling comes from." She quickly discovered that she was actually selling, and she was the only female in a male-dominated company. Her creativity kicked in and she put together a three-ring binder to showcase her products and quickly excelled, selling more than her male peers. Marsha's innovative product sales binder is an excellent example of doing it a little bit better than anyone else, of putting thoughts into action and taking risks, of silencing the voices in our head which say, "What will other people think?" "And I think all women, no matter how brave or brazen or confident or assertive you are, always have that stigma within us which comes from our teachers, our parents, and comparing ourselves with the other little girls we grew up with."

Fast forward three years. Marsha was asked to interview for a position selling yellow pages advertising over the telephone for GTE Directories Company. She took the job and within nine months was asked to accept a managerial position as a trainer, coaching people who had, in many cases, been there for years. "A mental fast track consuming knowledge," is how she described her next steps! "But, I am partially dyslexic and it let me know that I can, with focus, assimilate information very quickly. It's because I've had to trick my brain around the dyslexia." She stayed with GTEDC for fifteen years and advanced to executive management. She was then recruited by Westinghouse American Directory Project as an executive vice president in sales and marketing doing turnarounds, which she describes as her greatest business success. Marsha refers to this time as once again taking risks. She had to relocate from Southern California to Atlanta, which she describes as very different. She moved away from her mother, which was very, very difficult, but she says "it was the best decision I ever made. I knew inside it was best for me, for my mental growth, for my personal growth, and for everything else."

After taking personal responsibility to gain the financial wherewithal to do so, retiring early was Marsha's goal when she relocated to Arizona in 1990. She took a position with US West Yellow Pages, now Verizon, for another turnaround project. "I'm a very social person," Marsha describes herself, and after arriving in Phoenix, "I picked up the phone and called a friend and said, 'I want to get married again!'" Her friend was adamant that Marsha use a matchmaker in a time before eHarmony and other on-line services were widespread. It took her two years to finally pick up the phone and take her friend's advice. Giving herself permission to do something new, she took another risk and met Al, who became her husband and "her greatest personal success." Marsha shares this experience in her book, *Shopping For Mr. Right … because you don't have time for another Mr. Wrong.*

In 1992, Marsha retired as planned and a couple of weeks later her husband said "Get a job; I love you truly, but you're driving me crazy!" She had absolutely no clue what she wanted to do and interviewed to be a concierge at a mall, to run a maid service company, and to be a headhunter. Then she saw an ad about becoming a professional speaker and thus began the next stage of her life. She became a speaker for a public seminar company and traveled the world speaking as far away as South Africa, Australia, New Zealand and Europe. "It was marvelous," Marsha says, and then people from her corporate life began calling to request that she come back to their businesses and speak. One day Al told her, "You have a business going on here; you need to give it a name and incorporate."

When I die, I want people to say, "She gave back more than she received, and she always connected her head and her heart with her mouth. If I can help one person a month have a little bit better life according to them, not according to anyone else, I've lived my life's mission. I truly believe that the Lord has put us on this earth for a very particular reason and it's our job to figure out what it is that we were put here to do. I want to help people take personal responsibility for making better choices."

"Understand how you are perceived . . . it is absolutely critical," said Marsha. Young women today will tell her, "I'm not going to learn to play golf," and Marsha relates a story about her corporate days when she came to work one Monday and asked about scheduling a meeting to discuss a particular issue. She was told there wouldn't be a meeting because the men had already discussed the issue on the golf course over the weekend and made a decision. Marsha, a tiny but feisty dynamo, learned to play golf!

This passionate woman is as comfortable in the boardroom or speaking to large audiences as she is training at the firing range. She's an avid outdoor adventurer, she's passionate about living life to her fullest, and she loves playing golf!

"When I look back now over my life and call to mind what I might have had simply for taking and did not take, my heart is like to break."
— *William Hale White*

BE OPEN TO OPPORTUNITIES

Opportunities are everywhere! Even in a difficult economy opportunities surround us. We only see them if we are prepared and open and recognize the opportunity. Choosing to do something is what sets you apart and makes you a winner.

Have you accepted limiting beliefs about yourself? If you ever said, "I'm not creative!" or you failed to attempt a new activity or project because you feared someone may laugh, you are placing restrictions on your ability to see opportunities. Open your eyes and your mind to different possibilities. Do not become the person who "can't see the forest for the trees."

Pam Gaber Witnessed a Life-Changing Moment

Pam spent fifteen years in the corporate world working for a pharmaceutical company. She traveled constantly, often passing her husband in the airport. Then her inner voice said, "Is this all there is?" Knowing there was a different life out there for her, prompted her retirement. She began volunteering at the Crisis Nursery, a safe haven for children under ten years of age. She felt she needed to connect with her community and chose to work with kids because 'kids are fun'.

"Miss Pam, Miss Pam, what did Gabriel do this week?" Gabriel, the Weimaraner Pam had adopted, was the subject of many stories Pam told each week to children at the Phoenix Crisis Nursery where she volunteered. Little did she know, her pet was soon to become the spark that triggered the launch of an amazing organization. In one instant her life changed because she recognized an opportunity to do something special, and she knew she had to do it! Gabriel was one year old when Pam took him to a Christmas party at the Crisis Nursery, so the children could meet the wonder dog they had heard so many stories about. "Those kids were different that day! Kids that were angry and violent, were at that moment suddenly transformed. They were so amazing, loving, and kind. They hugged and kissed Gabriel. We all stood looking in amazement. He reached the children like none of us could." The director said, "I don't know what happened here today, but could you bring Gabriel back?" And since his calendar was relatively open, Pam did.

After researching, Pam realized there were no organizations in Arizona which met this need and Gabriel's Angels was born. "It started by accident, but it continues on purpose, and after eleven years, we now have 150 therapy teams and reach 13,000 children annually."

"Ten years ago, I would never have seen this opportunity. I would have taken my dog into the nursery and driven home. I would have been the same person," explained Pam. "So often things happen and we just miss it. We are so busy, we are rushing from here to there and think 'that was nothing' and we miss the moment. And the whole time the universe screamed, 'I showed you your opportunity, and you dissed me . . . again!' so I think it's about being open."

"Failure means I had an opportunity to learn something, and I encourage a culture of failure at Gabriel's Angels, as long as you learn from it. I've never been afraid to make the mistakes because that's my opportunity to learn." Pam delegates responsibility to her staff, knowing that they won't always do it the same way she would. She's very focused on the big picture and very clear on what she's not good at. She feels no pressure to be everything to everybody.

"I'm in training right now for something; I just don't know what it is," exclaims Pam. Her year of volunteering at the Crisis Nursery prepared her to recognize the opportunity and the need when she first took 'the little grey dog' to meet the kids. She just 'saw it' and knew what she had to do. Her corporate career trained her to run Gabriel's Angels as a business.

"I quickly discovered raising funds for a charity is a lot different than selling a widget. It was all about the mission. I wasn't asking for me; I was asking for the 'little people' and it's easy to ask if you believe in the mission," smiled Pam as she showed me pictures of Gabriel with the kids.

"When you find what it is you love, life is fluid. Every day you make a difference and you get up the next day and do it again! Time is seamless and it isn't the drudgery of a job. It's different for everyone and it's a zone you get into where life just flows," explains Pam.

Pam's advice to women in business comes from her personal experiences. Faced with Gabriel's death in May 2010, and her mother's death shortly after that, she found the inner strength to move forward. Pam was interviewed by the local television station the day following her mother's death because Gabriel's Angels was selected as their 'charity of the month' and she saw the importance of being there as part of the bigger picture. A plaque on the wall behind Pam's desk says "*Never, Never, Never Give Up.*" She thinks it's so easy for many people to give up, and many do just before turning the corner of success. Pam is passionate when she advises people, "not to cut off another person's head to feel taller yourself!" She believes in genuinely giving to others, taking responsibility, and not being a victim. She encourages women to 'trust their gut', because she grew up believing 'people are good' and discovered that it isn't always true. If your gut is screaming 'no', listen to it! That may bring confrontation, but with it an opportunity to learn.

"Be secure enough to show people who you are, be authentic, and let people see who you are. You can deem yourself a leader, but look back and no one's behind you! People choose to follow and aspire because you inspire them. They want to be better because you are a genuine role model."

Enthusiasm and humility best describe Pam. She frequently talks about the opportunities and recognizes them as they appeared in her life. She sees Gabriel's Angels Therapy Teams as an opportunity for people to work with their best friend while helping the neediest children. Her legacy is a foundation in Gabriel's name she started in 2000 to carry on the dream.

Pam tells Gabriel's story in her recently published book, *Gabriel's Angels – The Story of the Dog Who Inspired a Revolution*. It is a story of love and a story of hope for the future.

"Listen to your inner voice... for it is a deep and powerful source of wisdom, beauty and truth, ever flowing through you... Learn to trust it, trust your intuition, and in good time, answers to all you seek to know will come, and the path will open before you."

— *Caroline Joy Adams*

LISTEN TO YOUR INNER VOICE

At a very early age, few people know exactly what their purpose is in life or what they want to do in life. Some people never figure it out and continue living lives of quiet desperation. Others know they are not on the right path but haven't figured out what they want to do when they grow up. Some are fortunate to figure it out at a relatively young age and have the courage to pursue their dreams.

Michelle Medrano Rejected Her Inner Voice

"You should be a minister," a voice whispered as Michelle was sitting in a classroom. She turned around to see who said such a crazy thought. Her plans and goals were focused on the theater. She loved singing and performing. Michelle was in an Improv comedy group for a while, and she absolutely loved being in front of an audience.

"This career as a minister was a complete surprise to me. I didn't sit around as a little girl and envision that I was going to grow up to become the minister of a church. I was naturally curious about the universe and enjoyed going to church," she said, but Michelle had experienced a very tumultuous childhood that had an early impact on her religious path. "I lived with a lot of violence," acknowledged this serene and smiling woman I spoke with. "My father was a very violent man, and I remember my mother saying that the priest said 'to just be a better wife and he will quit hitting you.' I loved going to church, but I just couldn't agree with their take on our family struggles. When my mom finally found the courage to take her three children and leave my father, the church said, 'Well, you can't belong anymore; you're divorced'."

Michelle and her mother began looking for a new church and found an unusual spiritually-based church in Denver. Here they found the support and love that helped fifteen-year-old Michelle begin to heal from some of the pain of her past. Although Michelle loved this church that helped her let go of some of the struggles she had experienced and to see her life in a new way, she still planned to pursue a career in theater.

The summer between high school and college, Michelle took a series of classes at her new church. As she sat there listening to the instructor, she heard a voice say, "You should be a minister." Michelle remembers looking behind her to see who spoke those words. There sat a guy sitting staring back at her with an expression that said, "What's your problem?" It was disorienting, but she felt it seemed like some inner guidance. Michelle says she discounted the idea immediately as the dumbest idea she had ever heard. She was having fun working at different jobs in retail, and had just registered for her college classes, planning to major in communications and theater, and possibly pursue a career in broadcast journalism.

"Ministers are boring and stuffy and all they do is church," thought Michelle, "and being a minister is definitely not as sexy as being an actress. I couldn't even fathom it! My perception of a minister just did not match the desire in my heart for my career." Michelle remembers though that the experience had such a profound impact on her that she approached the teacher during a class break and asked how someone went about becoming a minister. She learned that in addition to being educated in the faith, there were many years of study required, and she still needed to complete her college degree. At this time there was a college in Los Angeles which she could have attended, but Michelle was only interested in going to Los Angeles to be in theater, not ministerial college.

Michelle recalls later sitting in one of her college classes thinking, "What does algebra and biology have to do with becoming an actor?" She continued taking classes at the church which she absolutely loved, describing a feeling of being 'high' when she was in the classes at church. This never occurred while attending her basic college courses, although she did enjoy the theater classes. Michelle was asked to try out for performances, and she did very well at that. About her second year of college, Michelle took a spiritual practitioner class which led to another profound moment she describes as a 'volcano erupting within'. The inner voice said, "Your life isn't about theater; your life is about the practice, the teaching, and the articulation of this." This was the moment Michelle says, "I almost fell down on my knees because I knew what I was supposed to do. It was a true moment of clarity. And I said 'alright, whatever I have to do, I'll do it.'"

Michelle was amazed when two weeks later, the minister of her church in Denver told her that they were going to be opening a ministerial college right on the Denver campus. Up to this time, Michelle had not revealed her thoughts to anyone because she was ashamed to tell people, and she really believed it was such a stupid, silly idea. She questioned, "Who am I to think I should do this?" She actually began working for the church, thinking the exposure would finally kill these thoughts. After working there for two weeks, Michelle decided she would never be a minister because they work too hard and were constantly sought after. She said, "There is all the glory of the speaking to masses and the recognition, but there are all the business aspects, the facility costs, paying the staff, dealing with the board, and all the things that didn't appeal to me at all!"

Michelle finally let go of her resistance and applied for ministerial school. She transferred all of her credits that she could, enrolled in the program, and began a journey that changed her life.

Michelle believes that all of us have an inner voice or intuition, if you prefer, that will guide us. Most of us simply cannot hear it with all the noise and distractions of our lives. We also all have gifts, skills, and talents to give back to the world. "I look back now and all the signs were there," says Michelle. "I loved the religious classes and did not enjoy many of my college courses. One of the challenges of figuring it out so young though was that I was twenty-seven when I graduated, and the congregation didn't take me seriously. I think I experienced the opposite of age discrimination; I experienced youth discrimination. How could they possibly learn from me because I was so young? People usually see their ministers as more seasoned." Michelle proceeded to do her job well. She patiently observed and learned while in Denver, and used this knowledge with her new congregation in Huntington Beach, California, after her ordination. At first she felt saddened and discouraged because she felt the congregation thought she didn't know what she was doing. Despite the setback, Michelle knew she had to keep doing what she loved, be true to herself, and prove herself. It took two years, but because she was patient, she earned respect in her new role.

Another intuitive moment in Michelle's life came after four years in Huntington Beach. She knew it was time to move on and find her own congregation. There were a number of openings she interviewed for in Northern California and two locations in Arizona. The Reverend, Doctor Michelle Medrano has been at home as the Community Spiritual Leader of the New Vision Center for Spiritual Living in Phoenix for fifteen years now.

Michelle came to this community wanting the members of the congregation to train her in the way they wanted her to minister to them. She had observed and learned from mistakes of other ministers. "I didn't want to be a *super hero* rushing in saying '*here I am to save the day!*' and change the work that had been done by the previous minister," Michelle exclaims. She observes that many people in business make a common mistake by not first watching the existing dynamics in an organization. She advises that you "observe what is already happening and what is already working. See what is already in motion before you change anything. You also establish trust when you vibrate at the same place where they already are. Then as you develop rapport and you begin to feel the ideas emerge for what you would like to see happen, you have fertile ground for making change. If you go into any business environment with the attitude that I'm going to do this and I'm going to change that, you miss opportunities to really transform businesses."

"I delegate, delegate, delegate, and let people in the community do what they do best, and I do what I do best. If I see that the community is becoming a little stale, one of the first places I look at is me. I check to be sure I'm not off track!" These qualities are vitally important to succeed as a leader. "If you are a business owner who wants to attract clients, or if you work for a corporation and want to move up, the degree to which you exploit integrity is sensed by others and is, in fact, repulsive to many. If we say one thing yet do something else, that negative energy is quickly recognized by others more than we imagine," states Michelle. She laughs and says, "I know where my strengths aren't," and is willing to get the support she needs. When I asked Michelle to define success, she very bluntly said that when she gets discouraged and thinks, "I don't have a mega church," she finds it is because she is comparing herself to someone else. True success for her is doing what she loves, giving the best gifts that she has, and feeling happy about it.

Learning to trust the inner voice took a little time. Michelle refers to it more as being obedient to it. Sometimes when we follow it, she muses, we are forced into an even greater challenge. We think something's wrong when we get to this really 'icky' place, but what's important is who we will become when we get to the other side. It's not easy. You have to do the work, you have to grow, and become something you aren't now. That's when the most powerful growth happens. "But the classes are so hard," she laughs!

Michelle is excited to have been part of the integration team that successfully reunited the United Centers for Spiritual Living and Religious Science International, which had been separated since 1954, but she has some decisions to make about her future. Michelle's goal is to have a role as an international leader in the newly integrated community and must determine the best timing for herself, her family, and her community. She has learned trust in her inner voice and finds peace knowing the answers will come to her when the timing is right and her mind is open.

The fun of entertaining an audience is still part of what she enjoys. She sometimes finds an occasional opportunity to be on stage at New Vision's Rubicon Café, for an evening of fun, food and song.

"The people who get on in this world are the people who get up and look for the circumstances they want, and if they can't find them, make them."
— *George Bernard Shaw*

HAVING THE COURAGE TO CHANGE COURSE

You are driving across town and make a right turn. You immediately hear your GPS system telling you to make the first U-turn and go back in the opposite direction. Don't you wish you could get such quick feedback in real life if you take the wrong path or aren't sure exactly which path to take?

Our school systems do not always do the best job of preparing us to make decisions in our life. Some of us are fortunate to learn from our family, organizations, or team coaches. But too often young adults head out into the world unprepared to choose their direction in life. I recently talked with an attorney who spent many years and many dollars acquiring her education and working as an attorney. She no longer found satisfaction in her work and was looking for a new path. After having made such a major financial and time investment in her career, she struggled walking away from it. It takes courage to make major life changes. Leaving behind the safety and familiarity of what you know and venturing into new territory can be frightening.

What is courage, but making a decision and acting on it?

Sally Horton Kelly Chose a New Path

Sally planned to study English and become a teacher. She always loved literature and English, so teaching seemed a natural progression for her. Following a class reunion I was unable to attend, I saw that Sally's email address on a class contact information book was "@columbia.edu". I immediately smiled thinking Sally had done more than just land a job teaching English. She had achieved the ultimate success becoming a professor of English at Columbia University. I sent an email to Sally to congratulate her on her successful career and to say hello to a former classmate who had attended the Girl Scout Senior Roundup in Coeur d'Alene, Idaho, with me in 1965. We had gone different directions in our lives and lost contact with each other. When I opened Sally's reply, I was not surprised to learn about Sally's success, but not as an English professor at Columbia as I had thought. After obtaining her Master's Degree in English at Indiana University, she decided she really didn't want to teach.

Sally stepped off the path of her original plan when a physician in her hometown was building a new office and offered her a job cataloging and establishing a library of their medical journals. She became very interested in reading the journals and described the experience as fun. Other factors came together to create a perfect storm in Sally's life. She was in a relationship, but he was serious and she wasn't. About this same time, her brother was graduating from medical school and she thought medicine was interesting. Coincidentally, a major Supreme Court decision would influence Sally's choices about her future. In 1971, in Reed v. Reed, the Court ruled for the first time ever that a law that discriminates against women is unconstitutional under the Fourteenth Amendment.

She made the decision to take a risk and do something completely different from her original life plan.

When Sally talked to the admissions board about going to medical school, she was told she needed additional science classes. She worked part time and got a loan, and she was back in school. After completing this additional year, she was unsuccessful getting admitted to medical school. However, Sally was determined that was not going to stop her from attaining her goal. She enrolled in a master's degree program in Medical Genetics. The next year she successfully gained admission to medical school, and she began a course of study that would culminate in her medical degree.

But choices and decisions were not over for Sally. While attending medical school, she worked and studied with a resident in psychiatry. Sally loved psychiatry and this would have been her first choice when deciding which specialty to choose for her residency. But, out in the real world, women needed access to obstetrics and gynecology specialists. In the 1970s, this was still primarily a male-dominated field.

Once again outside factors impacted her career decision. Sally met her husband while he was working on his Ph.D. at Indiana University. Upon graduation he received a job offer at City University of New York. During her junior year of medical school, they moved to New York City and eventually found a place to live in the Village. She switched her specialty and was accepted in an obstetrics and gynecology residency at St. Vincent's Hospital in New York. Sally says, "This was a good choice" and she's loved her career.

Sally faced challenges which are not always apparent to others. Moving and living in New York City was difficult in some ways for her. Being from the Midwest, she didn't know the geography, had no family or local connections, didn't feel a part of the New York history, and endured many Midwest jokes.

With change sometimes comes opportunity. When her husband had an opportunity to teach in Paris for a year, Sally enjoyed a year off work giving her the ability to explore the beautiful city and all it had to offer. Sally cherished this time with her three-year-old daughter.

As we talked about taking risks during her career, Sally was quick to point out that those risks opened new opportunities for her. She said she might also have taken another path at one point in her career when she developed an interest in surgery, but the challenges of having a child during this time made it difficult to manage the rigorous schedule that would have been required. Later on, she entertained the possibility of pursuing administration rather than continuing her clinical practice, but chose to continue her private practice. "If only" is not part of Sally's vocabulary, and she shares that she loves her career and the rewards it brings to her life.

Sally's work brings her into close contact with women from all walks of life. She says, "Basic life demands often determine where you are in your personal journey, and you may feel you don't have the luxury of changing. But if you are not happy with what you are doing, have the courage to change."

"I certainly don't regret my experiences because without them, I couldn't imagine who or where I would be today. Life is an amazing gift to those who have overcome great obstacles, and attitude is everything!"
— Sasha Azevedo

CHANGE YOUR ATTITUDE . . . CHANGE YOUR LIFE

Your attitude is the key to where you are and where you will go in life! Understand that it is not the event; it is your attitude towards the event that makes the difference! Believe in the value of programming your attitude!

Begin every day with a personal goal that will open your mind to possibilities, welcome opportunities, and bring joy. Your attitude determines your ability to experience success and happiness.

Developing a positive attitude requires controlling the input you receive and controlling what you tell yourself. Hearing someone say, "You can't do that," requires you to say, *"What makes you the expert?"* before deciding if you will accept their input!

Do you ever say, "I knew that was going to happen?" when something negative takes place in your life? Be aware of all the things your brain is saying to you throughout each day. Every time you catch something negative, stop and reprogram your thoughts to a positive one. A positive attitude will make the impossible . . . possible!

Kyna Rosen Learned This Lesson Early

"You have diabetes," were tough words to hear from her physician at age fifteen. Kyna immediately wanted to know how it would impact her participation in sports and what foods she could eat. Knowledge about managing diabetes was not as extensive then as it is today, and when her dietician said, "You can't do that," Kyna's immediate reaction was, "Watch me!" For the past twenty-three years, Kyna has lived with Type I diabetes and proved not only to herself, but to others, that her attitude made her a winner. Following her initial diagnosis, Kyna craved more information about the impact diet and exercise would have on her life. The list of foods she could not eat was long, and one dietician discouraged her from exercise that could complicate managing the diabetes. Most people without health challenges never run a marathon in their lifetime, yet Kyna ran five marathons one year, wanting to see how far she could push herself. Eliciting her physician's support, together they developed a plan to adjust her insulin and allow her to see what was possible. She was so committed to reaching her goal that right before the Big Sur Marathon, which she was scheduled to run with a team of friends, she received an opportunity to interview for a great job. Accepting the interview would require her to fly out of state and miss the marathon she had trained for intensively. She made a choice, which some people in her life questioned, to run the marathon. "It turned out to be a great decision," she says, "because I then got a really good job offer from a company that was more of a fit. I chose to put my personal health and goals first."

Kyna's success managing her diabetes for twenty-three years has inspired her to help others, and that passion is evident when she talks about her work. She is a health coach, fitness trainer, and the head

Kangoo Jump instructor and rebound shoe dealer/distributor at Kangoo Club Arizona. Her clientele ranges from young children to a 109-year-old man who asked her why she challenged him to try Kangoo Jumps. With a big grin Kyna said, "Because I knew you would!" It's all about impacting clients and how she makes them feel. She is passionate about building strong relationships with them and gives them tools they can use for a lifetime. Kyna is committed to meeting her clients where they are in their life, and she will help them adjust their habits so the changes are gradual and attainable. It's not a diet . . . it's a lifestyle change.

Kyna tells me that from the time she was eight years old, she wrote down her goals for the upcoming year. She laughingly told me about a contest at her school where the person selling the most popcorn would win a radio with a headset. She really wanted the headset and radio, so having observed her father in his sales job, she got out the phone directory and started cold calling people in her neighborhood. At age eight, she had no fear and she was number one in popcorn sales. She believes if you really set your mind to it, you can do it. You just have to make a commitment.

She continued to push the boundaries and be open to life's adventures. While attending college, Kyna had an opportunity to study in Israel. Focusing her energy, within two weeks she applied for and was accepted at two schools and awarded two scholarships. Kyna wanted to stay in Israel for six months rather than the one month program approved by her school. To do so, she had to withdraw from the university she was attending. She subleased her apartment and went to Israel, and was later readmitted to her university.

Kyna's body of work has focused on health and fitness. She teaches her clients to take baby steps forward as they learn new habits. Success is different for each one. If a client eats donuts, she teaches them to switch to eating half a bagel instead, and then to substitute an English muffin. She helps them plan a "food budget," teaching them one step at a time how to develop healthier habits. Kyna works closely with her clients to help them learn personal accountability, which is a key to lifelong change. "Face everything and avoid nothing" is the philosophy she teaches. "It's not going away, so you might just as well face it now and decide how to handle it. My diabetes wasn't going away, so I had to work on myself. By doing that, I could then help others."

"If you're not having fun, you're doing it the wrong way," is how Kyna describes you should be doing everything in your life! She advises that you discover what your true passion is, and hold that vision for yourself. Even if you have to take a few side jobs before you get to your dream job, stay focused on your long term goal and know that you can make a difference. "Find your gift and share it with others," is a message Kyna wants people to embrace. "It doesn't do anyone good if you have a gift and don't share it. Sometimes we don't even realize the impact we have on other people's lives."

"Life is like running a marathon, and you need to have a plan. If you want to run twenty-six miles, you break it down into realistic goals. We don't always realize the potential we have, because we don't break it down to make it attainable."

When Kyna discusses her work, she is excited that she was asked to design and implement several sixteen-week wellness programs for communities that have a high incidence of diabetes and obesity. She offered them many different fitness and nutrition tools to help them take their health to another level while still having fun doing it.

One of Kyna's visions is to do more work with children to help in the prevention of obesity and diabetes. "Have Fun Getting Fit" is Kangoo Jump's message for all age groups.

Kyna discusses her legacy and her commitment to make a difference in the world. Helping people to change their lives and experience the results of taking better care of themselves is her goal, and she is committed to making a global impact. As her network expands, she envisions taking medical supplies and education to third world countries in the future.

Your attitude says, "I am a success!" You don't have to ask for permission. You can be the person you want to be. You must ask yourself, "What does success mean to YOU? . . . not anyone else . . . it's your life!" You can write the story. YOU are the star. Remember that it is YOUR story.

"Go confidently in the direction of your dreams. Live the life you have imagined.

— *Henry David Thoreau*

THE WORLD STEPS FORWARD
WHEN YOU ASK FOR HELP

Life isn't always perfect. Actually, life is rarely perfect. In fact, it is sometimes so impossibly difficult we don't believe we can ever achieve our dream life. Obstacles can seem overwhelming, and we often think if we ignore them, they will just go away. The truth is they won't. The challenges are different for each individual, and we must each find our own path. The wonderful news is that we don't have to do it alone. I am reminded of *The Wizard of Oz* and the journey the tin man, the scarecrow and the lion took to find a heart, wisdom and courage. It takes courage to ask, but that step can change your life forever.

Holly Hunter Asked for Help

"My heart is soaring! If I can keep doing this stuff, I know I am doing what is my bliss!" Holly was grinning as she described a recent outdoors hiking and camping event she had coordinated. She described the fun and enjoyment the other families were having while spending quality time in the outdoors, and she said her reward is seeing their happiness.

Just eighteen months ago Holly was not smiling. "She's in the waiting area, but she's in tears," one of the Fresh Start staff members told me. Holly had come back to the women's resource center to meet with me in my role as a volunteer career coach. I met Holly recently when she attended a workshop I facilitated at the center. She realized that she needed help getting back into the workforce. Describing her situation, Holly says, "I imagine I didn't appear to be the 'normal' client who walks through the door at Fresh Start, if there is such a thing. I have a bachelor's degree, I lived in a 4,000 square foot home in a nice part of town, I'm well dressed and I had a spouse who made a six figure income. But this is where the facade ends. I had a great deal in common with the many women I met at Fresh Start. I am going through a divorce and I was completely terrified as to how I would survive financially. Being an unemployed stay-at-home mom for the past seven years had been extremely fulfilling but did little for my resume. I needed ideas for getting back on my feet after being cut off financially as punishment for filing for divorce. I was lost, lacked self-confidence, and felt I had nothing to offer. Who would want to hire me? I was especially overwhelmed at the idea of drafting a resume and was literally frozen with fear and had trouble moving forward to take the next step. My first visit to the center gave me a renewed sense of hope. It was so wonderful to know that these amazingly positive women were there to offer guidance and not judgment." The center was there to support Holly, but Holly had to do the work.

Holly knew all about facing challenges and doing the work. She has lived a life most mothers do not wish for their daughters. Holly went to Wichita State University right after high school. She was a little sister in a fraternity and partied a lot, had a new boyfriend, and did not do very well that first year. She dropped out and moved to Vail, Colorado, and became a ski bum. "It made my parents crazy," Holly said. She did return to Wichita and went to summer school and tried college again, but she just wasn't doing well. "I tried to kill myself when I was twenty," Holly revealed. She had a history of depression and intentionally overdosed on Tylenol. "It was the second attempt," she said. "I had tried earlier when I was fifteen by taking some muscle relaxers," she shared. "It was a cry for help both times. My parents were so totally shocked because I had kept everything inside. I was a cheerleader, a straight-A student, I was on student government, and I was a super high achieving teenager who was messed up on the inside."

She started seeing a psychiatrist after the first suicide attempt, and he released her after about a year and said she was fine. "But I never really felt fine," Holly emphasized. "I went back to school but I was still partying. I even wrote a letter to my mom to ask for help, but I took the letter back out of her purse before she read it."

"I had lost my virginity and then my boyfriend immediately dumped me. I ended up in a tailspin and I started drinking when I was fourteen years old. I think it was a problem for me from the very first drink I took," Holly told me. Being date raped in college was now part of her experience and her 'out of control' life finally led to her second suicide attempt. A month in a lockup unit was next in her life and they tried to convince her she was an alcoholic. Holly emphatically said, "That's not my problem," but by age twenty-one she had a DUI. Her parents gave her the "shape up or ship out" ultimatum, so she left and went back to Colorado. Holly found a new boyfriend and promptly got pregnant. He wanted nothing to do with parenthood, so Holly moved back to Kansas. Living with her parents was not an option, so Holly found a job and learned to become self-sufficient. Holly admits to quitting her job for a short time and going on welfare; then she discovered a program that paid for child care for her infant son while she worked. She decided to go back to school for a couple of years but when she was not accepted into a nursing program she quit school, met her first husband, and got married. That marriage ended in divorce after four years. Holly returned to school and finally graduated at age twenty-nine.

Holly moved to Arizona with her new fiancé and gave birth to her second son before getting married a second time. Holly describes herself during this time as a "supermom," totally available to her kids. She involved them in numerous activities and sports, and Holly somehow felt that the number of activities she enrolled them in was a measure of how good she was as a mom. She kept a beautiful home, cooked delicious meals, worked out at the gym, ran three marathons, and had lots of close friends. It might have seemed to others that Holly had the ideal life, but she was unhappy. Her husband traveled extensively for his job and their relationship became different, one she describes as "like roommates." Feeling overwhelmed by her life, she drank more and more to deal with the stress others didn't see. One glass of wine became two, then a few or a bottle. She didn't deliberately "hide" her drinking; she simply found ways to control it around others. Only she would slip up occasionally and do something embarrassing that she would have to explain away. Holly says, "Life just seemed less overwhelming once I had a glass of wine in my hand. At some point, I started to realize I could no longer say I was the best mother my kids could have; there was something seriously lacking. I would sometimes drive the kids after having a few drinks, I would lose my temper easily, or I'd wake up with a hangover and lack the motivation to really engage my kids. I was filled with resentment, anger, blame, self-contempt, irritation and mostly SHAME."

When she drank through her third pregnancy, "I knew for sure I was an alcoholic," Holly said. Her relationship with alcohol continued. "Even in the first trimester I would have a really large fishbowl glass of wine, saying, 'It's only one glass', but knowing it was two. I just couldn't stop even knowing it wasn't good for my baby." The last time Holly drank was at a Phoenix Suns basketball game she attended with a girlfriend. "I was driving and told myself I would only have a drink or two and I would have time to sober up before driving home. I had a lot to drink, and at halftime they wouldn't readmit me to the game. I told my girlfriend I was too drunk to drive, so she drove. I remember we stopped and got shakes at a drive through, which I spilled on the leather seats in my husband's new car, but I kept passing out. During the long trip home, I woke up and saw she was driving across the lines on the highway. She told me that was the only way she could see to keep the vehicle straight. Right after that, I puked all over myself and all over the car." Holly made it home, tried to clean everything up, and went to bed. The next day when her husband asked what happened in the car, Holly lied to him. As the day progressed, however, she kept vomiting and knew she needed to go to the hospital. Her husband took her and just dropped her at the entrance and left. Sitting in the hospital room, Holly said to herself, "I'm done . . . I can't do this anymore. And that day I was done. I asked for help . . . I knew I couldn't do it on my own."

Holly remembers one earlier time of wrecking the family car. She stopped drinking for a while, but her husband told her he "missed his drinking buddy." She tried to control her drinking for a while, but went back. After her trip to the hospital, Holly began a ten-week outpatient program, found an Alcoholics Anonymous sponsor, and worked through the steps. "There is no question in my mind . . . I am an alcoholic," Holly can now admit. "I've been sober over five years now and I still go to AA meetings, but I know I will never drink again!" Holly recalls losing friends who were "shocked and couldn't stand watching me sober up, thinking how could this 'supermom' be an alcoholic. I wasn't as 'crazy fun' as before, I stopped measuring my success by superficial standards, and I became a better mom, growing closer to my kids as we spent more time together camping and being outdoors." Holly wants women who find themselves in a similar situation to ask for help and understand that there are a lot of people out there willing to support you in whatever you are trying to do.

"I deserve better!" When Holly decided to ask for a divorce, she had gotten past blaming others for her situation in life. AA taught her that when you think others are at fault for what's going on in your life, it is time to look in the mirror. She is a survivor and knows she can and will do whatever it takes to provide for herself and her children. Holly's legacy is for her children to know she found ways to be better connected with them because of her love.

With her life now on track, Holly is in a new relationship. One day before they were actually dating, her boyfriend Rich said to her, "You're an angel, you know. All of the things you are doing for all of these families are making such a positive impact on so many children's lives." Holly formed Active AZ Families, and she organizes many activities where families can enjoy time together in the outdoors. She treasures a journal that she carries with her for the participants to comment on their experience. Reading their comments and knowing how much fun they had is so important to Holly . . . "more important than money," she shares! Someone recently told Holly that "people are lucky when they are around you . . . when they are in your wake!" Holly, who describes herself as an "adventurer," loves helping others who are not as adventurous learn to have fun and reconnect with nature. Holly blossomed as she discovered her passion. This confident woman knows where she's going and is taking along families having fun in her wake!

Holly advises women to never give up on their dreams and is following her own advice as she works to accomplish hers.

SECTION III

WHAT'S HOLDING YOU BACK FROM REACHING YOUR POTENTIAL?

"So oftentimes it happens that we live our lives in chains and we never even know we have the key."
    —*Lyrics from Already Gone,*
        Performed by the Eagles for their 1974 On the Border Album

WHAT'S HOLDING YOU BACK FROM REACHING YOUR POTENTIAL?

"I can't do it!" cries the little voice inside you. That voice is your greatest enemy. It creates the doubts and uncertainties that keep you from really going for it. Challenge yourself to yell back at that little voice and say *"Why Not?"*

Self-limiting beliefs can evolve into negative thought patterns. Over time, these thought patterns become habits that we often don't recognize we have. As you learn to identify and then challenge these beliefs, you will gain an understanding of the impact they have had on your life. You will also realize that you have the power to change those thoughts and beliefs. As you build new beliefs, you will revolutionize your life.

If you never step out of your comfort zone, how will you ever catch a glimpse of what is possible? It can be extremely frightening to try something new and different. Your family and friends may think you are nuts, or you may not believe you can do it because of a past failure.

In your mind, you may have created a long list of reasons why you can't possibly succeed, but consider for a moment that those reasons may not be valid. If they are not valid, they are just excuses to keep you from trying.

Identify What's Holding You Back

Rank these in the order of importance to you with '1' being the most important factor and '10' the least important.

_____ Fear of Failure

_____ Fear of Success

_____ Lack of Confidence in Yourself

_____ Lack of Time

_____ Lack of Necessary Skills

_____ Lack of Education

_____ Can't Decide Exactly What You Want to Do

_____ No Capital to Start Your Business

_____ Negative Feedback from Family/Friends

_____ Afraid to Take Risk

_____ Other Reason Specific to You

Once you rated their importance, let's take a look at your *#1* reason for not moving forward. Determining the greatest obstacle holding you back is the first step in changing your life. Once you recognize the barrier, you can then begin to develop a plan to overcome it. For example, if a lack of confident speaking and presenting your ideas to others is the reason why you are not moving ahead in your career, business, or life, you can begin by taking small steps to build your self-confidence. Try going to a networking event or a Toastmasters meeting. *These people are strangers and you will never have to see them again if you choose not to.* Prepare a brief thirty second description of who you are and what you do, and practice it aloud until you are very comfortable saying the words. Talk to your bathroom mirror and watch your expression. Remember to smile! Continue to place yourself in situations where you will use this new skill, and remember to congratulate yourself as your confidence grows. Apply this technique at every opportunity, and as your skill increases, you will notice more people want to talk to you and listen to your ideas. Begin visualizing yourself confidently talking to others, presenting your ideas to your boss, or promoting your business products and services.

Imagine how it will feel when they respond positively. Choose to be excited and enjoy the feeling.

You are beginning to shatter your personal barriers!

"If you are not doing what you love, you are wasting your time."
— *Billy Joel*

Do What Excites You

Most of us grew up with the belief that we should get a good education, become an employee of a good company, and life would be "happy ever after." Parents, teachers and other influencers in many of our lives forgot about the very different personalities we have and that some of us just don't make great employees. Even if we do make good employees, it may take us a long time to discover exactly what we love doing and are so passionate about doing, that it doesn't seem like work. The challenges for us arise when we haven't been encouraged to explore the many opportunities available to us as careers or businesses. We go off to college, decide on our area of study, graduate, and accept a job simply because we need to start earning income. It happens every day, but you don't have to stay there forever!

Gelie Akhenblit Didn't Like Going to Her Job; Sound Familiar?

"I am an extremely hard worker, but I am not the best employee," Gelie describes herself with a smile! "It's challenging for me to be at my desk on time every morning, and I have trouble working on someone else's schedule and dealing with that kind of structure. I had a 'cushy' corporate job and a great income with lots of potential" she says, "but I wasn't happy. I dreaded going into work every single day. It's not that I was lazy; I just didn't fit the mold and it made me feel bad about myself. I didn't know what else to do, so I started networking to find out what my other 'career' options might be. The thought of updating my resume made me sick to my stomach. I just wanted to meet other people and see what else was out there. I remember coming home from my very first networking event and feeling a 'networking high.' You know how your whole body is happy and you have a permanent smile on your face and the endorphins are pumping? I didn't even know what just happened, but I knew this is what I need to be doing. I just completely fell in love with networking."

Little did Gelie Akhenblit know that her love of networking would be the first step in her personal journey of discovering and living her dream career. It would also change her life forever.

In October 2008, Gelie launched NetworkingPhoenix.com with the goal of mobilizing the business networking community in Phoenix around a single collaborative platform. In less than three years, her idea of having a centralized events calendar has become Phoenix's leading online resource for business owners, entrepreneurs, and professionals looking to connect locally. At the core of NetworkingPhoenix.com is a robust, comprehensive, and free-to-use online calendar with a complete listing of business networking events, mixers and seminars scheduled in the Phoenix Metropolitan area (avg: 600 events/month). Since its inception, NetworkingPhoenix.com has skyrocketed in popularity while quickly becoming one of the most visited websites local to Arizona, and making an international imprint as one of the top 1% most visited websites globally. Over 17,000 members have joined in this short time frame and the website continues to build critical mass with approximately 530 new members signing up monthly.

"The question I get asked most frequently is to tell the story of how I came up with this idea. And the truth is that as I was networking, I found it very difficult to keep track of when and where networking events were being held so I started keeping a Word document listing them." Gelie very quickly acquired a reputation as the person to call or email for information about upcoming events. At this point, she wasn't looking for a job or asking anything of people at these networking events; she just enjoyed meeting people and her network quickly flourished.

In December 2007, Gelie's manager told her she needed to increase her hours at work, and at that moment, Gelie immediately decided to quit. "When the words left my mouth, I felt completely free," Gelie said. "I called my husband and told him to get our finances in order because I had just quit my job. It was really scary for me but also extremely exhilarating. I was in my mid-twenties and it was not just a job, it was my career that I was quitting. Best decision I ever made," she says with a giant grin on her face.

Gelie's fast-growing network was full of business owners and entrepreneurs. Very quickly, people began asking her to introduce them to others, to help them find seed money for their ventures, to network for them, or to help them find sponsors. Gelie decided to create a networking events calendar along with these four services for the Phoenix area and launched the Gelie.net website on January 1, 2008. "I didn't know the first thing about having a business and the first site was just a reflection of my personality; it was pink with a big pink flower as the logo," she reminisces. It had the calendar of networking events with four basic services. In the first month on her own, Gelie had four clients. "However, I quickly realized that I had just created another job for myself, only instead of one boss, I had four; and, I had a lot more work and was getting paid a lot less. I realized pretty quickly this was not what I really wanted to do, and I decided to keep searching for that right fit."

Gelie's epiphany came in somewhat of a unique location, but nevertheless, it was definitely what she was waiting for. Lounging in a poolside cabana in Las Vegas with her girlfriends, Gelie thought "who are these people that can afford $10,000 cabanas, and more important-ly...why am I not one of them?" With this lingering thought in mind, upon returning from vacation, she decided she had to create a company that could be duplicated and marketed many times over. "I should be able to drop it into any city in the United States, or even possibly internationally, and watch it grow." So she scrapped everything, except the calendar, got rid of the pink website theme, and NetworkingPhoe-nix.com was born.

Someone suggested she host a launch party when she relaunched the website, and Gelie decided it was a good idea. She sent out a few email invitations and reserved space for 125 people; to her amazement and everyone else's, over 500 networkers showed up! "You have got to be kidding me," she exclaimed. "But it put me on the map." Today, NetworkingPhoenix.com's Signature Event is held quarterly and much anticipated by over 1,500 attendees. At the first few events, people asked if they could purchase a display table. Initially Gelie said, "No", but they persisted and eventually she said, "OK, if you really want to pay me." Now the Signature Events are a significant money maker for the company and sponsorships sell out every event. "I don't try to sell anyone anything. I give them the information and, if they buy, they buy. It's very exclusive now and we sell out of spots fairly quickly. We are very fortunate to be in this position considering the current economic climate."

Gelie is passionate when she says, "You need to put yourself in the path of opportunity. You are successful when you reach and surpass your goals. Many people that I come across often don't have a vision to have those goals," she advises. "I meet a lot of entrepreneurs and many have a lot of ideas, broad ideas, but not always very specific goals. So it is going to be very difficult to measure success without those goals."

Gelie is also a big proponent of developing a strong team. "We are nothing without our support system. I would not be who I am without the people in my life that support me," Gelie told me. "I would not have the confidence that I have, and it's a very humbling thing to know that once that system is gone, everything you know can be gone very quickly. It's crucial to stay grounded and remember why you are where you are and never forget where your support comes from." Gelie urges women to build a strong team and avoid negative people in their lives. "Have a good mentor or a role model to look up to," recommends Gelie.

Gelie attributes her success to her love of people and her ability to connect with them. She builds and nurtures relationships and says "I've always had a passion for people and found a way to affect them on a daily basis. I had to find the right avenue to express that passion. I meet so many people with amazing skill sets, but they end up in industries where they can't use those talents. I want to tell them to follow their dreams, but I also know it's a very challenging journey. Sometimes it's all about creating space for opportunities and then taking them. I work my butt off every day to put myself in the path so when opportunities come up, I'm right there taking them."

Gelie always felt she would be successful, but she wouldn't talk about it to just anyone in her younger years. She, like so many people, needed that first win to develop the confidence to keep moving forward. She takes risks, but calculated risks, and believes in building a very strong foundation. It forces her to move slower, but avoid cracks in the foundation. "I have to make decisions for the business on a daily basis, and many times I don't know anything about the topic I'm making decisions on. But having had some 'wins' under my belt, I have the confidence to do what needs to be done," she says.

One of the challenges Gelie faces is working together with her husband in the business. "We have to be husband and wife, and we have to work together. We have to make time for ourselves and for our friends and find a balance that works. He is still working another job that he loves, but I plan to recruit him full time for the business one of these days," she says with a devilish smile. Challenges come with being an entrepreneur, "but I don't think my biggest challenge was growing the business, it was maintaining a somewhat normal life while birthing this idea. The first two years of the business were brutal. You pour heart and soul into it trying to be successful, all the while trying to make time for life."

Gelie also recognizes she wouldn't be where she is today without the support of her husband. "It's not all rose petals," she laughingly says, "but he's supportive and that's the #1 most important thing. He's there for me, and allows me to do the things I need to do for the business. My greatest personal success is being with him for over eleven years.

What I've accomplished so far, tells me there is nothing I can't do. I feel like if there is anything I want to do I just say, 'Gelie, what is it you want, write it down, put it out in the universe and make it happen.' "

Gelie, a Soviet refuge who came to the U.S. at the age of eight, describes herself as "accomplished." She's a daughter, a wife, a sister, a friend, and a businesswoman. "I'm also a mother, an author, and a national icon," says Gelie knowing that her vision of her future is already real. She just doesn't know the exact timing yet for each of those roles to manifest in her life. Gelie leans forward as she shares her goals and dreams with total confidence and belief. Connecting people, helping people, and giving them a tool that lives long after her by allowing them to come together and connect is Gelie's wish. "If I can help them find jobs, meet their next biggest client, put food on the table, or meet other like-minded individuals, I am helping. There are so many people out there that are lost, and if I can give them a roadmap, then I've done some great work here." This is the legacy Gelie wants to leave behind. She is passionate about the people, and for her, it is always about helping others. Truly connecting with them is a secret to her success.

As we get ready to go to press, Gelie learns she has just been nominated and selected as a finalist for the Greater Phoenix Chamber of Commerce Young Professional ATHENA Award. This award honors Valley businesswomen for their excellence in business and leadership, exemplary community service, and their support and mentorship of other women. The women honored not only excel in their careers, but make an incredible mark on the community where they live. At the annual event two finalists will receive the ATHENA Businesswoman of the Year Award and one finalist will receive the ATHENA Young

Professional Award. Gelie smiles as she talks about the success of NetworkingPhoenix.com. Pivotal times in her business growth made it impossible to turn back, but these times also allowed Gelie to see a larger world out there. "Once you see it, you can never go back!"

"It's not who you are that holds you back, it's who you think you're not."
— *Author Unknown*

TRUST YOURSELF . . . YOU ARE EXTRAORDINARY

Do you trust yourself enough to put your future in your own hands? That can be a very frightening thought for many people. Past failures come rushing into your thoughts and erode your confidence in your abilities. Most people have not had family and friends constantly telling them how extraordinary they are and what amazing things they can do. In fact, the opposite is usually the case. Many of us have experienced laughter and ridicule at our ideas and aspirations. We have not learned the value of the lessons in our failures; rather we focus on our failure. Life is all about experience. Begin today forgiving yourself for past mistakes and cheering your accomplishments. Begin to believe you are not only extraordinary, but you can trust yourself.

How Janet Brooks Learned to Trust and Use Her Gifts

"I was a free spirit with no goals and no aspirations for a career! In my twenties, I was a ski bum in Crested Butte, Colorado, and had no focus," Janet reflected on her past. "I was raised in a very strict Pentecostal family environment, and my father honestly believed he was a prophet. He was always preaching and prophesizing that the world was going to end in 1985. I never totally bought into all the religion; I felt like I wanted to believe, but it never felt right to me. I always felt like I was a little out of the loop compared to the other kids in the church. I honestly didn't think that I believed my father's prediction that the world really was going to end when I was in my thirties, but apparently at some level I did. I had listened to his preaching for so many years that the quotes from the Bible must have become a part of my subconscious beliefs. I had no focus to my life; I partied a lot. I was having a lot of fun. I never thought seriously about having a career. Why should I? The world was going to end," Janet recalled.

During her twenties Janet was employed in a variety of jobs, sometimes as a waitress, a bartender, or keeping books for small businesses to support the lifestyle of a ski bum. Finally, getting a little tired of this lifestyle, Janet found a job where she began to manage a design showroom, and she discovered a love for the design business.

Then at age twenty-nine, Janet broke her leg. It was a serious injury and she found herself in a situation where she could no longer support herself. She knew she was going to have to move away from Crested Butte. At this same time, a wealthy, older man wanted to date Janet and, since she had nothing better to do, she began seeing him. Janet shared, "I let him work his way into my heart. He was a really great guy, and I ended up marrying him."

"I had no consciousness yet that I was going for a career in interior design." Janet describes a trip to visit her mother, and while there, she looked through an old trunk filled with memorabilia her mother had saved. Janet came across an old paper she wrote her freshman year in high school about what she wanted to be when she grew up. She had no memory of writing then that she wanted to become an interior designer.

Her father told her many times during her youth that, "You are going to Hell if you do this, you can't do that, you aren't good enough, and it was all negative, negative, negative!" This left Janet with a little voice inside that sometimes tells her that she's not good enough, that others are better or more skilled, or that she's too old, or she doesn't have political or social connections like some of the designers, so she's not getting the good jobs. Janet has learned to focus on the positive and believe in herself. She surrounds herself with proof of her success as a reminder of all she has accomplished.

Janet's journey has not been an easy one. She recalls her first design business and describes the shock of returning from a business trip in Denver and finding that her partner had locked up the business and had taken all of the money. Janet had looked up to this partner as an expert, and she couldn't imagine herself running a business on her own. She felt completely unqualified, but realized there was some design business out there solely for her since her former partner was leaving town. Janet tortured herself making the decision to take on a project with seventeen condos, each having a different owner. At first, she said, "Who am I kidding?" but she finally said, "I can do this!" She successfully took on the project and said, "It gave me a lot of confidence."

Janet's challenges were not over. When her second husband wanted to move to Arizona, Janet left behind a very successful design business in Durango, Colorado. Her husband built spec homes at a time when Arizona's economy was booming, so they relocated to Scottsdale. Janet had not planned to work after the move. She had been pregnant with her first child when she moved to Arizona and helped her husband with his business. She now wanted to have a second child and although her husband agreed, one day he came home and told her he was in love with another woman and left the next day. She had absolutely no clue this was coming. She was living in a half million dollar home and believed they were doing fine financially. What she learned shook her to the core. Not only were they significantly in debt, her husband had stolen money from investors. As he walked out the door, he told Janet that if she wanted to save her credit, she would have to pay the bills because he planned to declare bankruptcy.

At this time Janet's mother was her dependent, so they had to sell her mother's house and move her to Arizona. Janet describes this time as extremely difficult. Emotionally she was trying to recover from her husband's deception, and she had to find a way to support herself, her child, and her mother. She only had about $3000 to her name. "It was urgent," she said. "I couldn't take a year to figure out what I was going to do." To make matters worse, my husband showed up, took my car, and gave it to his new girlfriend!" Janet used her mother's old Subaru for about a year. She immediately started looking for a job as a designer, knowing she couldn't start a design business. She had no capital and no business contacts in Arizona. After many interviews and repeatedly being told that she would have to bring her own clients with her, she realized she had no other alternative but to start her own business. Every morning she got up at 4:30 to go to areas where nice houses were being constructed. She knew developers always came by to inspect the projects, so she brought her portfolio with her and asked about doing design work. A smaller developer building $250,000 homes gave Janet her first job, and she earned $500 for each home doing colorization--

not what Janet considered 'real' interior design work--but picking colors and tiles for the homes. Slowly, she started getting more work, and today Janet is still here in the same area doing what she loves.

Janet's showroom contains many awards celebrating her success in the design field. Her company, Janet Brooks Design, has been featured in numerous magazine articles, most recently in Arizona Foothills Magazine.

"I see the world in patterns and colors and everything around me is like a photograph," describing how she gets her inspiration. "I walk through the world very aware of everything, light and color, hue and texture. I don't consider myself very artsy; I can't even draw; and because I didn't go to college for design, I can't do AutoCAD (computer aided design). I see my job as meeting with clients and getting inside their head to understand their needs and what they enjoy. I look to my talented design assistants to execute the plans."

Janet believes in doing everything to the utmost. She strives to be the best at whatever she does. "When you're in the position of having to be the breadwinner, you either go and hide in a corner or you get out there and do what you have to do." Following the end of her second marriage, Janet remained single for eleven years and was responsible for rearing and supporting her son. She had to trust in her abilities as a designer and as a salesperson to build a company that would provide for their financial needs.

Janet wonders whether she would have had the drive to do what she did if she had had someone to fall back on. At the time, she had absolutely no one to help her, and had to do it herself. She says, "This was a gift for me, because I got to find out who I am." Janet believes that when parents help their children too much by paying their bills and helping them out, they are not really helping because their children never get to learn who they are and what their capabilities are. We have many resources within that we don't discover until we are tested.

Belief in yourself is a quality you need for success. Remind yourself that you've done it before and trust yourself to do it again. Janet advises, "Don't compare yourself on the inside to someone else's outside. It's easy to feel like we are less than someone else, but we are all talented, and we all have resources, and we are all going to make it if we believe in ourselves."

Janet learned to trust herself and her success today is a reflection of her clients' trust in her skill.

"Progress always involves risk; you can't progress to second base and also keep your foot on first."

— *Christie Mason*

TAKING RISKS

One of the world's greatest risk takers was Christopher Columbus, who sailed across the ocean not knowing what he would find at the end of his voyage. We don't have to undertake a journey of that magnitude in our own lives to discover success. We must, however, sometimes travel in uncharted waters to move forward with our lives. Learning to take calculated risks is an important skill that can keep you ahead of your competitors and allow you to win your personal Success Game.

As you make decisions about your life, your career and your business, take the time to evaluate the potential positive and negative outcomes. For example, if you think you deserve a raise or promotion at work, what might you lose by asking for it? Your boss could say 'no', but that is probably the worst that could happen. If you plan well and develop a strategy before talking to your boss, you could get exactly what you ask for.

Taking risks in your business, career, or life can make the difference between great success or massive failure. You lessen your potential for failure and improve your potential for success by understanding how to take calculated risks. The key factors to evaluating your risks are:

- Explore the possibilities
- Be thorough in your research
- Weigh the risks
- Be willing to fail
- Learn from your failures
- Develop your strategy
- Implement your plan
- Monitor the results
- Be prepared to make adjustments

Begin today taking the first steps on your personal path to empowerment and success. You will gain courage with each new step you take.

Marie O'Riordan Risked Following Her Dreams

"Every day . . . I'm a thrill seeker! I freak out if I'm in a comfort zone," exclaimed Marie when I questioned her about taking risks. She describes herself as "Tigger" *and* the "Duracell Bunny." She works hard, plays hard, and is so passionate about her work that passion oozes out of her pores! Marie embraces life and says she knew exactly what she wanted from an early age. She has been working in radio and TV since age thirteen and was a Sony Award winning short filmmaker at age fifteen. By age twenty her career had taken a quantum leap forward as a journalist for CNN. At twenty-two, Marie was the last person to be granted an interview with Mother Teresa, the Nobel Peace Prize Winner, just prior to her death in 1997. Marie has just been nominated for The Entrepreneur Leaders of the World Award 2011 in Monte Carlo, and is Europe's #1 Media Marketing Expert.

Marie has been taking risks and shattering barriers her entire life. Born in Ireland, she was the youngest of four children. Her parents encouraged her dreams and instilled the belief that Marie and her siblings could accomplish whatever they wanted. They not only set no limits, but applied no pressure. As a result, Marie and her siblings are a "force in the world" and each is at the very top of their respective industries. Her parents tell her they laughed hysterically at the things Marie came home and said she wanted to do, which at one time included her plans to drive the space shuttle! Their support and encouragement gave Marie the confidence to pursue her personal dreams.

Marie encourages people to recognize the 'dream stealers' in their lives. Many people have a dream, but the people who are the closest to us and should be the most supportive, laugh at those dreams and ultimately make us afraid to pursue them. "I am acutely aware of the people I hang around with, and the people I choose to allow into my life. If someone is a bad influence in my life, I cut them out," Marie said as she discussed building her personal support team which she believes is a crucial key to success.

For Marie, discovering her passion was "like a light switch went off in my head. The path was laid out, I think, before I was born. I was following the path of broadcasting, and someone gave me a chance. It just clicked and I knew from the first time that I broadcast, that I would be doing it for the rest of my days."

Marie began to pursue her personal dreams when she focused on getting her education in journalism and radio, and by age thirteen, she started broadcasting. Her career had an exciting advancement when she began reporting for CNN at age twenty. Marie was very good as a journalist, and her expertise in her workplace environment at a very young age caused some of her colleagues to feel threatened. She was a female competing in a male-dominated field, and she had to work very hard to earn respect as a journalist. "For many years I was the only female broadcaster in the entire organization. I know what it's like to break through barriers and have the people 'upstairs' watch what you're doing. Sometimes it isn't a very pleasant place to be, but I knew I was good, I knew I was talented, and I knew I deserved their respect," Marie shared.

She believes that, "Anything is possible for people if they work hard." Marie frequently asks people if they hit 'snooze' when their alarm clock goes off. She laughs and says, "That tells me where they are in their life, and it must be a pretty darn boring life if you have to hit the snooze button!"

"Belief . . . absolute, total belief in whatever I wanted to do" is how Marie describes her life. Her mother told her she started talking about things she was going to do in her life at an early age. She didn't realize they were goals until she was older. About age seven, Marie told her parents that she was going to hang out with Mother Teresa. Marie told me, "It took me until I was twenty-two, but it happened. From the time I was a young child, anything I ever wanted to achieve happened. I have become so good at manifesting and am so clear with my visualizations and my goals, that now, when I see something, it's done. This comes from my total belief and absolute one hundred percent certainty that what I believe and what I want is done. I just have to catch up in time!"

"This can be a scary thing for some people to hear because they don't feel that they can do it. Also, they don't have that belief in themselves. It can be very intimidating for people who may not be as confident and who don't believe they have that ability. But they do. In fact, every single one of us has a shining star inside," Marie smiles as she shares this belief.

Marie discusses taking risks and she says she takes calculated risks. "I will step outside the boundaries when it comes to news stories, but I won't compromise my ethics or endanger lives. I like to push the boundaries because when I step outside my comfort zone is when I have the most growth. And when people say, 'You're crazy; it won't work,' then I know I'm onto a good thing." She has taken many risks while traveling on her personal journey and says the rewards have been unbelievable. Her journey has also taken her to many third world countries, both to film hard-hitting documentaries and as a volunteer.

Marie has been doing volunteer work since she was fourteen years old. A cousin who was only two weeks different in age than Marie, died from leukemia at age four. "It was like losing my twin," Marie remembers. Her little cousin had been treated in a French hospital, and Marie decided she wanted to volunteer in hospitals and began her volunteer work at this same hospital. Marie has an enormous passion for helping others and continues today to do extensive volunteer work in third world countries.

Thinking back, Marie said that most people don't know that Mother Teresa had trained in Ireland, Marie's home country. From the time she was seven, Marie had a strong belief that the two of them would eventually spend time together. An alignment in the universe placed Marie in India in 1997, volunteering in the slums of Calcutta.

She describes rescuing babies from a train station and trying to help in this enormous city with a population of twenty million people and terrible sanitation conditions. A chance meeting with an Irish nun the day before Marie was scheduled to fly home and a chain of circumstances gave Marie the unbelievable opportunity to interview Mother Teresa in her Calcutta home, the last interview she gave before she passed away. Marie said Mother Teresa's message was both simple and powerful: "Every single person is special, and no matter what they have done in their life, they have the potential to be good." She considers interviewing Mother Teresa one of the most memorable and moving highlights of her life.

Marie's path has also encompassed many challenges and obstacles in both business and her personal life. She has faced difficult health issues, including dealing with extremely debilitating migraines, but she remarks, "It's a little thing called life! We all have challenges. The important thing is how you deal with them. You always have a choice," Marie says. She decides what she puts in her body and what she allows into her mind. Eating healthy foods and supplements and avoiding caffeine are instrumental in taking care of her body and allowing her to function at her highest level. She applies the same criteria to her mind and says she is always learning.

As she pursued and lived her dream career, Marie said, "I have pinched myself so many times to be sure it is really happening." Marie earned much success in her professional life. "It's a load of baloney!" Marie comments about the original definition she learned for the word success. Through the wisdom she has gained along her path, she learned success is a lot more than bright lights and the bling. "Success is in the small little things and in what I'm able to do for other people. I take myself out of the equation because it's not about me. It was never about me; it was about the people I could touch, the audiences I could move. But more than that, it's also about spending time with the people I love. Next week I will get to spend twenty-four hours with my mom! I'm not going to get to do that again for five months, so for twenty-four hours that's my success. And every day it's different."

Marie looks forward to a future that includes a vision of building her legacy to the level of her dreams. Those dreams include building schools and hospitals around the world and "touching people and inspiring them, in turn, to touch and inspire more people, because that lives on."

"You can have anything you want if you will give up the belief that you can't have it."

— Dr. Robert Anthony

LET'S BELIEVE FOR A MINUTE YOU CAN DO IT!

How exciting are the possibilities for you! Belief is the key that changes everything. You must be totally convinced you can do it, and you must feel deeply convicted that that confident woman is who you are. When you see yourself living your dream and begin to believe it's possible, things start coming together to make it reality.

Kimber Leigh, Award-Winning Actress and Producer, Believed

Kimber Leigh came to Arizona knowing she was going to become somebody else. Over an eighteen-month period, two of her brothers had committed suicide and her mother began to drink to kill the pain. Eventually alcoholism killed her. Kimber knew she had to leave Pittsburg and start fresh. She says, "I was running to a new life that offered more opportunity."

Kimber always told her mom she wanted to be a flight attendant and a famous actress, and her mom had actually given her a book on how to become a flight attendant. In a world where some people do not believe that coincidences happen, Kimber rented a house in Phoenix from a man named Ed Beauvais. When Ed came by to maintain the lawn, he used to tell Kimber that he was going to own an airline someday, and she would respond, "Sure, just like I'm going to be a flight attendant and a famous actress!" Then one of Kimber's friends saw an ad in the newspaper for a company hiring flight attendants. Her friend was aware of Kimber's desire to become a flight attendant and sent in an application for her without Kimber's knowledge. Kimber received a letter asking her if she would interview for the position. Five thousand people applied for 121 positions. Kimber immediately decided she absolutely had to be in this first training class. She interviewed, but was notified that while she didn't make the first class, she would be considered for the second class. Kimber ripped up the letter while telling herself that she just had to be in the first class. Four days before the first class started, she received a phone call saying that four people had failed their exams and asked if she was interested in joining the first class. After doing cartwheels in the living room, Kimber was ready to begin training for the career she always wanted.

She went to orientation and was surprised to find Ed Bouvais, then the CEO of America West Airlines, the country's first deregulated airline, welcoming the first class of flight attendants. Kimber thought to herself, "Wow, he did it!" and she went on to have a fulfilling twenty-one year career which ended September 11, 2001. Kimber had already been informed that she had been the flight attendant on a 'dry-run hijacking' flight with an al Qaida terrorist prior to this date. She was out on disability from an injury on September 11, 2001, when she received a phone call at home about the three hijacked planes. She turned the

TV on and collapsed watching the coverage, knowing then her career with the airlines was over. She knew she couldn't live in fear and go to work every day looking over her shoulder every moment to see if terrorists would hijack the plane she was on.

The year before the hijacking, Kimber somehow understood that she wasn't destined to remain a flight attendant for her entire life. She had already begun doing some acting, and searching for avenues to start developing an acting career. Arizona is obviously not Hollywood, and Kimber asked God, "Why, if acting was what you put in my heart, did you put me here in Arizona?" She knew moving to Los Angeles to pursue an acting career was not in her heart. Continuing her search, she saw an ad for extras in the movie, *Leather and Iron*, which J. Archer Productions was filming in Arizona. The director, James Archer, and Kimber bonded as friends and he invited her on set as often as possible to enable her to learn. They shared a passion for Phoenix and for filmmaking and although James passed away two years ago, Kimber fondly remembers his passion for this industry and the support he gave her.

"I couldn't go on being an extra in films for the rest of my life," exclaimed Kimber, "so I took a job bartending." One day while working she noticed a poster on the wall that said "I'm living my dream . . . do you want to live yours?" Auditions for another movie were going to be held in the bar where Kimber worked, but she was scheduled to bartend during the audition hours. "Really, God, now how does this work? There are a hundred people here to audition for this movie, and I have to serve them!" Kimber could not let this opportunity pass her by, so she asked one of the waitresses to talk to the director and see if she could audition as the very last person since she was working. Her boss agreed to her plan as long as everyone had been served and the audition didn't take too long.

Kimber was one of the last to audition and the director asked if she could scream. Kimber said, "Gee, I don't know. . . I've never had to in my entire life." She delivered a couple of lines and then it was time for the scream. She closed her eyes, prayed, and then she let out this horrific scream. Everything around her went dead silent. After what seemed like forever, everyone started cheering. Kimber didn't get the part. Undeterred, she called the director and told him that he had to hire her. She said, "I am that person; this is my only chance. I have a dream and you have a dream. Your poster said 'share your dream with me,' and you are never going to find anyone with more passion. Please hire me!" He hired her. The film was shot in Colorado in late October of 2005. The temperature was about ten degrees during filming. Kimber was running through water and climbing up mountains, soaking wet, dressed only in a tank top and jeans, which resulted in severe hypothermia. But she gave this opportunity everything she had to prove she could do it. The film is still sitting in the can. "So here I am again, asking God, 'Now what?' " In 2006, the same director called Kimber about an upcoming film festival called *The Almost Famous* and told her he thought they should enter a film short. It was a forty-eight hour challenge where you write a script, shoot, edit, and submit a film. Of the sixty-four films entered, they won three of five awards. That's when her career took off. "I could have given up many times, but somehow life wouldn't let me. It kept giving me another opportunity and another opportunity."

Constantly looking for different paths to her dreams, Kimber had been doing fitness training. She entered a Miss Fitness competition where she placed third in the western region which qualified her for the national competition. She had been training for four years when six days before the event in Las Vegas, she ripped four muscles off the bone in her hip. Kimber truly believes that you "NEVER give up," so she went to Las Vegas for the national competition on crutches and encased in a cast from the bottom of her foot up to her hip. She knew she looked good. It was a body building competition and she put on a two-piece bathing suit, went on stage and showed them what she had worked hours and hours over four years to accomplish. She felt that if she showed up on stage on crutches she could spread the message, "*Do Not Give Up!*" She was disqualified from the competition because she was not able to perform the routine, but she was awarded the title, "Miss Fitness USA." Kimber thought fitness was going to be her avenue to success as a print model or spokes model, but that ended with her injury.

Kimber's father, the son of Czech immigrants, is her greatest inspiration. "My father watched his two sons, his wife, and his brother commit suicide, and he never gave up. He loved life! Near the end of his life and very, very ill, he went on every vacation he could. He just kept going." He passed away in late 2010, and Kimber says the lessons she learned from him have influenced her decisions and her ability to believe that she will accomplish her dreams.

Reflecting back to when she was only about five years old, Kimber recalls standing outside her home in the snowy streets of Pittsburgh. Looking at the windows of the homes around hers, she remembers saying to herself "Why, Lord, why am I not living in that house? At that moment, it was almost like a light was shining on me and I really knew what I was supposed to do with my life. I knew I would be protected, and I knew what I would do, and I believed that I was put here to make a difference."

Discussing the very public recent meltdowns of celebrity actors and actresses, Kimber says, "The film industry needs valid role models. You become more of who you really are the more exposure you get. The person you are becomes bigger. I'm not twenty years old," Kimber laughingly says, "but I'm not dead either, and there is nothing wrong with being a role model at any age. I'm not the norm for this industry, but there's no reason I can't become the norm." Kimber says one of her greatest obstacles was not the way she looked but the way she spoke. "People would look at me and think 'big boobs, blonde hair, she has to be a *bimbo*'; but if they took the time to talk to me, they would say '*the package doesn't match the verbiage*.'"

"I shouldn't be where I am at today because there was roadblock after roadblock," Kimber shares. When *VROOM* was first filmed, the director told her they weren't even going to edit it. Kimber was persistent, constantly calling about the film. After months of putting up with her calls, they finally threw it together quickly and gave it to her, saying "here, it's yours!" She turned it into an international award-winning film short, and today is coproducing and staring in *VROOM! The Movie*. Kimber says "If you don't believe first, how would anyone else believe in you? If you believe, no one on this planet can stop you."

As Kimber looks to her future, she draws from her past. When she was young, her grandfather bought a vanity set for her and sat her down to look in the mirror, telling her, "Honey, you're going to Hollywood." He pointed to a picture on the wall saying "you're going to be just like her." When her father passed away, Kimber returned to Pittsburgh. Her brother told her that her grandfather always wanted her to have the two pictures hanging by her vanity set. She took a picture of them with her cell phone and showed them to her husband who was curious about the signature on them. He blew the signature up and said, "Do you know who this is?" The signature was Mary Pickford's, the first silent screen actress and founder of the Academy of Arts and Sciences.

Thinking about her dreams, Kimber says, "Why can't I be the Mary Pickford of independent films? Independent films are becoming top winners at the Academy Awards now!" Kimber is passionate about bringing the industry back to the basics and showing that quality films can be made to entertain people and can be made without multi-million dollar budgets.

Kimber wants every woman to hear this message: "Don't look for your self-worth and self-value in a man. Love yourself regardless, even if your hips are big or your toes are small. Embrace who you are . . . your mind, your body and your spirit. If all three are working together, your package is complete. Believe in yourself first and no one in the world can stop you!" She says, "Remember to look for the gift in every bad experience. The people who annoy you the most will be your teachers. Once you find the gift in obstacles, they move! You think it . . . you create it! Thoughts are things!"

"I haven't lived my dream life yet . . . but I'm on my way," Kimber exclaims! She has now worked in over thirty-five film shorts, five full feature length films, producing ten of them. Kimber's awards include four as outstanding actor, one for ensemble acting, five as a producer and numerous awards as a correspondent. Her latest achievement is directing *Questions*, a film short debuting in the fall of 2011. In addition to pursuing her acting career, Kimber is active in her community with organizations such as the Phoenix Volunteer Group which assists in the development of shelters for women. In the future, she hopes to speak to aspiring actors and actresses so they can learn from her experiences and not give up hope when someone tells them they can't do it.

"People with goals succeed because they know where they are going."
    — *Earl Nightingale*

THE POWER OF SETTING SPECIFIC GOALS

You have heard many of your family members and friends make statements about the things they were going to do. Depending on their individual situations, it could have been "climb Mount Everest" or "find a job." One of them may be planning to start a business, or just lose twenty pounds. Regardless of their plans, most will not achieve their goals without developing a well-planned strategy and action plan. If your goal is too far out there and too large, it is easy to become overwhelmed and find yourself doing things that will derail your goal. People who are successful in achieving their goals, take the time to break the big goal down into manageable, smaller goals. They plan exactly what they need to do, when they need to do it, and put it on their schedules. Each day they review it to see if they accomplished what they planned, and they make sure they review their priorities as they move closer to their goal.

Julie Armstrong Wanted to Work for Jobing.com

Julie Armstrong is currently in transition. She is not willing to settle for just 'a JOB'. She is looking for a career opportunity that she can be passionate about. Julie knows how to search for jobs. Her background is human resources. She has a plan that includes very specific criteria that she will use to identify the company she will work for next.

You are probably wondering how Julie ended up in her current situation . . . unemployed, or to be more politically correct, in transition. She knows all the secrets of job searching and getting hired. But as we all know, life sometimes gets in the way of our plans. We must make choices. More recently, when a situation arose with Julie's parents that would require a significant time commitment from her, Julie resigned from her job and went to Ohio to care for her parents and help them transition into the next stage of their life.

After accomplishing that, today Julie is back in Arizona. She knows how to set goals and make them happen. When I met Julie, she was the Community Relations Director for Jobing.com, an Arizona job search website. She was conducting a workshop for Jobing.com about using the many resources available on the Jobing.com website. Her enthusiasm for her job and her company was contagious, and she shared the fact that she was working in her personal dream job.

Prior to that, Julie had worked in the human resources department for a financial institution that was a client of Jobing.com. Working closely with Jobing.com allowed Julie to observe the corporate culture and she liked what she saw. While she wasn't unhappy at her company, she wanted to work in the type of environment she saw at Jobing.com, and set a goal to become their Community Relations Director. Did she have experience in community relations or sales? Definitely not! But

Julie had something equally important . . . passion. She told herself, "That looks like something I can do!" She was passionate about her desire to work for this company and was determined to make it happen. Julie knew it was totally uncharted territory and asked herself how she could get there. The knowledge that she did not have the right background was a potential obstacle, but Julie kept her eyes on her goal. "Never think you cannot do something . . . try it first, then decide," Julie recommends. She worked at building relationships with the Jobing.com team over a very long period of time and when the job offer finally came, both Julie and Jobing.com wanted to work together. Recognizing her enthusiasm, Jobing.com agreed to give her the training and support she would need to learn the online job board business and succeed.

Julie succeeded and her four years working at Jobing.com led her to a new passion. She became very involved in community outreach and volunteer programs and took on leadership roles in numerous community organizations which she continues to pursue to this day.

Julie talks about her decision to leave Jobing.com to help her parents, "who are the reason I am who I am today." She describes her mother as a trailblazer back in the 1960s, who was working full time, getting her college degree, and involved in caring for her family. She was a woman who was ahead of her time, recognizing the importance of work/life balance. Julie attributes her outlook on life and the person she is today, to her father and her mother. "Their values: integrity, work ethic, family and friends first, and a positive attitude, set my foundation early on," Julie said. It was important to Julie to help her parents transition successfully into the next phase of their life. She knew it would take longer than a twelve-week FMLA leave of absence, but this was her family, and she was committed to helping them for as long as it took. It took six months, but during this time Julie never stopped her volunteer work in the community, never stopped her community outreach work, and never stopped her leadership roles in the organizations she was working with.

What's next for Julie? She pondered this question for a moment and smiled. "I'm looking at doing some consulting and some coaching, and I will finish the book I've been working on for two years. I don't know what will be my next career stop. It may be human resources, business development or sales and marketing . . . or a combination of all of them." I asked Julie how she will decide on the company she goes to work for. She is very specific about the criteria she will use when selecting this company, and she uses three areas for evaluation when making her decision. "The environment and culture of the company must be a match with my ethics and integrity," says Julie. "I want to know how they are with employer/employee relations, and I want to know about their community touch. If all of these align with my values, I know I will have the work/life balance that is essential to me."

"It's okay to ask about the company culture in interviews," Julie emphasized. "Don't settle! It's better to take three to six months interviewing and searching for the right position with a company that is a good match for you versus accepting a job and staying for a year just to pay your bills. If you do that and leave, you have just lost that time in your life. It is also important for you to make a plan for your job search. If you have to take a part-time job to meet your financial needs during your search, do that, but don't lose sight of your goals." Julie strongly believes that everybody possesses something unique that some employers want, and encourages you to keep searching for the right job.

"We're all way too good to settle," she says, "and sometimes when you're in it, it is very hard to see outside the window past your challenges. It is hard to see that tomorrow will be better, but if you don't start believing that tomorrow will be better, it never will. I think it's really important to find a mentor or join a support group that can hold you accountable," and Julie shares that she personally has several people, including her mother, who hold her accountable.

Julie also advises there should always be someone in your life--a boyfriend, spouse, a coworker, a mentor, a friend, or someone who is in your life and knows what you're about and what you are doing--to keep you in check. She is adamant that you surround yourself with positive people and suggests if the list of negative things about a person exceeds the positives, you remove that person from your life.

Julie says that getting divorced was the best thing that ever happened to her. She is now stronger and more independent because it forced her to get out there and do what she had to do to move forward with her life. She says, "You have to find the positives within the negatives and ask yourself 'what's going to be best for me, and what do I want out of this?' "

Success to Julie is doing what you say you are going to do and carrying it through to completion. It's not about the tangible things; it's about work/life balance and enjoying life and all it has to offer. "I have a vision board," she mentioned. "If I have something on there that I know I can't complete in six months, I take it off and put it on the back of the board until the next time. I know some people say you should leave it on there, but it's a distraction to me."

Julie had no thoughts of success when she began working in human resources at a dry cleaner in Ohio. Her goal was a new car. She had no vision of becoming a human resource director for a large company. As she moved on to a financial institution and started thinking outside the box and received some accolades for what she was accomplishing, she started to believe she could do something more.

As we discussed the things that contributed to Julie's success, she was thoughtful as she mentioned integrity first, but she also stressed the importance of trust, both in yourself and in others. "That's a hard one, being true to yourself and trusting in yourself," she says. "I never let anything defeat me. I've had a lot of personal challenges and a lot of things happen that were unexpected." Julie quietly shared that a close personal friend's fourteen-year-old son had passed away four years ago in a bicycle accident. Learning to share the family's grief and celebrate his life taught Julie that you find support in unexpected places and that you cannot ignore challenges . . . you must face them and move forward. Julie believes you must "let go of the things you cannot control. Your #1 priority should be to manage your personal outcomes, and everything will fall into place."

"I'm the consummate networker," Julie describes herself and attributes her success to networking and building relationships with no expectation of receiving anything. "Build the relationship and things will come to you," she says. "Let people know what you need and want, but don't use people. Share what you want and need with people and if they have the resources, they will reach out and help you." Julie thinks, "It is also important to listen to people's needs, as well. You may be able to assist them in ways you never imagined. This is the 'building' part of any good, sustainable relationship."

"I haven't lived my dream career yet, but I've had a lot of great steps. I know where I'm going! I don't want to miss out on anything."

As we go to press, Julie is beginning her new job at Phoenix Job Corps. Her goal, to be worthwhile and use her skills and background to benefit others in her community, matched perfectly with the opportunity. Phoenix Job Corps serves over four hundred students, ages sixteen to twenty-four, teaching them the skills to succeed in today's workforce. As a volunteer employer while at Jobing.com, Julie served as the chair of their Industrial Advisory Council. Her relationships, reputation, and community involvement made her an ideal candidate for the position, and one of seamless transition for Julie.

"An expert is a man who has made all the mistakes which can be made, in a narrow field."

— *Niels Bohr*

MASTER THE SKILLS AND BECOME AN EXPERT

Mastering a skill or acquiring significant knowledge about a subject is one of the most valuable assets you can have. Being an expert is marketable at many levels. You can be the expert in your local business community or international business community and be assured that customers or clients will seek you out and pay top dollar for your services. You can also be the expert in any given area within your corporation and be rewarded with bonuses and salary increases. Research and discover the very best people in your area of interest. Read, study, and learn everything you can from them. Observe what these experts do and follow their example. Share this information. Teach what you have learned, and your skills will grow as your students demand more of you. Your sphere of influence will likewise grow as your expertise grows.

Tracy Repchuk Is an Internationally Recognized Expert

"You will never survive in a job!" Tracy heard these words from a business teacher shortly before she graduated from college. Her classmates were sending out resumes and getting ready to move to

Toronto to begin their careers. Tracy didn't have any idea what she wanted to do. Her business teacher had pulled her aside to discuss her future and told her, "You are a leader. You are far too powerful to be a worker." Tracy said, "That moment changed everything for me. There is a little advice here for each of us, especially for those people who are successful. Planting little seeds like that can have an enormous impact for someone, because it did for me. And at that moment I said to myself, 'Wow, I don't have to go out and get a job; that's what my parents wanted--for me to get a job. I still remember the day I went home and I said to my mom and dad 'I'm going be an entrepreneur; I'm not going to get a job.' My mom cried. She thought I was throwing my education away. So that was a very interesting turning point for me, but it was a moment when I knew I could never be an employee."

Today Tracy is the 2010 Top Woman in the World for Internet Marketing and the World's Number One Passion to Profit Expert. She is the bestselling author of *31 Days to Millionaire Marketing Miracles*, and an international speaker and motivator. As an expert in her field, Tracy will tell you that finding her passion and excelling in her field didn't just happen by accident. For the first twenty-seven years of her career, her work was not her passion. One day when Tracy was about forty years old, she was sitting there thinking and said, "This is not enough. I'm not contributing to society and I'm not out there helping. I need to start searching for something that excites me and allows me to be a contributor to the world."

Soon after, Tracy went to her first internet marketing seminar and her world shifted. Two things happened: she knew that this was what she wanted to do, and she would become an internet marketer and show others how to succeed in what they were doing. She also saw that there were no women speaking on the stage at the seminar, and that planted another very important seed for her. Tracy was off and running! She had found her passion.

"Yes, I did!" was Tracy's reply when I asked her if she always knew she would be successful. "But I have experienced failure," she replied. She shared the experience of her fiancé announcing a week before her scheduled wedding that he was leaving her for someone else. Devastated, Tracy soon married someone else at a time she admits was not optimal. Although the marriage lasted only nine months, the person she had married fought her for half of her company and her house. He closed her credit cards and wanted her to pay alimony. And then her business partner and former fiancé decided to fight for the other half, changed the locks on the business, and cut up the business credit cards. Suddenly, everything Tracy had built was gone. Everything she had created, even her security, was gone. She moved home with her parents to try to figure out what to do next. "That was the biggest challenge I ever faced," says Tracy.

Taking risks along the way was something Tracy says she did frequently. She 'rolled the dice,' but says that they were always calculated risks. She always asked herself, "What is the worst thing that can possibly happen? In most cases it wasn't that much . . . there are far bigger deals." Not running off to Toronto to take a computer programming job at graduation, starting her own business at age nineteen, leaving Canada and moving to the United States to start a business, and later leaving her business to go into internet marketing were all risks. She says, "I don't worry about the consequences to the point where I'm not functioning and doing what I'm supposed to be doing. I always feel that if I'm not risking something and if I'm not a little scared or out of my comfort zone, I'm not doing what I'm supposed to be doing at that point in time. She believes that whatever you think you're capable of doing, in reality you're capable of far, far more. It's scary to take a jump sometimes, but that's when the rewards are the biggest."

"I was always responsible for me; I was going to choose the outcome in my life. I watched people I admired, those that did whatever it took to get what they wanted." Tracy shared that she closely followed exceptional athletes at the time, and individuals like Bill Gates and Steve Jobs. In observing them, she learned important lessons that she embraced in her own life, one of which was spending twenty hours a week on personal development. Tracy emphasizes that "your mind is a very powerful thing, so if you know you're going to be something, you're probably right. So I've always maintained a positive attitude and taken the steps to carry me toward my goals."

Setting those goals high and staying focused on them was a key to Tracy's success. When she saw the opportunity in internet marketing, she wrote and launched *31 Days to Millionaire Marketing Miracles* in fifty-eight days. She recognized the need for a book on the topic, her content was relevant, well written, and it was an overnight bestseller, generating six figures in revenue in the first five months online. It has been in the top four percent of books sold on Amazon for the last four years. With her book's huge success, Tracy launched a coaching career that got her noticed by the World Internet Summit, and resulted in her winning New Internet Marketing Success of the Year. The Summit paid all expenses for her to go from California to Singapore to appear in front of her first audience of over 3400 people which automatically launched her into her next stage as a platform speaker. This is where

Tracy says, "You don't always need to know the *how* ... just launch what you want and stay true to your path, and the *how* gets solved. I never could have pictured a start like I got. It was way beyond, resulting in a quantum leap that never stopped."

When I asked Tracy what made her unique, she replied, "Everyone is unique! What I've done in my life and with my life . . . I am *me*! You have to bring your uniqueness into the business world. If you don't, you lose the ability to communicate as *you* and you become robotic. At that point you become a pawn in the system and you lose your ability to make an impact in the world." She explained that her uniqueness really developed over time and suggests you look back to when you were a child and see what you were like. She was strong and a leader even as a child, but there was also a period when she was almost crushed. Tracy learned that when you are very successful, there are always people who want to see you fail. She feels staying authentic to yourself during tough times is of vital importance. She discovered that if she looked for a need in the marketplace and filled it, it was someone else's need, and she wasn't passionate about it. But "when I turned it around and said, 'I want to help other people uncover their passion and teach them to make money doing it,' that is when I really discovered my uniqueness." And that's her tagline, 'The World's Number One Passion to Profits Expert.' "

An internationally recognized expert, Tracy sees herself as an ordinary person who has managed to implement some key strategies developed by some very clever people who went before her. "I have the ability to follow what others have done and not attempt to change it until it's been mastered."

Getting there isn't always easy. Tracy's career has seen many ups and downs. "You can't predict some of the things that are going to happen to you or the economic situation we are all getting pummeled with now. But, you can predict how you react to those situations, and that is what really determines success."

Becoming an expert has given Tracy success that is individual to her. She says, "To do what I want, when I want, and with the people I want to do it with, is success to me. My work is fun and I love to play. I spend my money on experiences. I want to build great memories of vacations and time spent with my family."

Tracy's story has not ended, and she tells me her newest ventures result from meeting other world renowned experts and joining together, combining their talents to offer something that they could never have done separately. She believes when you partner, there is a level of empowerment that emerges as experts join together to help others achieve success.

"A champion is someone who gets up when he can't. "
— *Jack Dempsey*

BE A CHAMPION AT BUSINESS AND AT LIFE!

Champions! This word brings to mind the Super Bowl, the World Series, the Indy 500, the Academy Awards, the US Open, Wimbledon and more. Excitement, the thrill of winning, being the best, and all the emotions, recognition and money that comes with being a champion are not exclusive to the events I just mentioned.

Being a champion means being the absolute best at what you do! That does not mean you have to be a sports hero or famous actor/actress. It means *BEING THE BEST AT WHAT YOU DO!*

If you are thinking "But, all I do is . . . work for a company in an ordinary job," stop those thoughts right there! I am going to say it again—being a champion means being the absolute best at what *YOU* do! Champions inspire and motivate people, and generate enormous excitement when they perform. Their skills are honed to a level most people cannot imagine, and they make a commitment that most people are unwilling to make. Champions choose not to be average.

What are their secrets? The secrets are actually simple. They are not easy, but they are simple.

Secret #1: Create the vision and the desire. You must be able to see yourself as a champion and really believe you are a champion. This belief must be so strong that nothing can knock you off course. It does not matter what reality looks like today, you know in your heart you are a champion.

Secret #2: Champions do not settle for 'good enough'. They seek perfection in their performance, and they work every day to improve their skills. They practice and practice and then do it again. They analyze their performance, review it, and make corrections and adjustments. Then they practice again and again. Champions work to achieve perfection and they don't stop until they achieve it.

Secret #3: Champions persevere. They know there will be failures. They know how failure defines you. Champions fail and then they get up and do it again. Each failure brings them closer to success.

Secret #4: Make sacrifices. Champions do what others won't. They push their bodies and their minds beyond the limits where most people are willing to go.

Secret #5: Champions believe in their success. They know they are champions and no one can do what they do better!

Believe you can accomplish great things! Believe you are a champion!

Valerie Thompson's Quest to Be the Best

"Tell me what to do and I will find a way to do it better," announced Valerie Thompson, the Two-Time Land Speed Record Holder at Bonneville Salt Flats. She is a champion, both on her motorcycle and in her life. She says, "Dreams happen on napkins," and she has a collection of napkins and coasters with handwritten notes tracing the history of

ideas and thoughts that came to her in restaurants and bars. She also keeps a small collection of wine bottle corks on her desk with significant reminders penned on them which she studies until she 'gets it.'

Valerie tells me about "life at 200 mph", but it wasn't always like that for her. Her first invitation to ride a bike came from a gentleman who "kept his bike so clean and polished you could eat an egg from it. When I got there to ride on the back, he withdrew the invitation because he was afraid my jeans would scratch the bike." He said, "You know, Valerie, girls do ride by themselves." She said, "I always had a thing for motorcycles; I just had never been on one before. So he took me down to the Harley Davidson dealership the next day, and I bought my first bike. The dealer was in Bellevue, Washington, and I lived in Tacoma, and was afraid to drive it home."

Valerie's grandparents were a significant part of her life and they told her that she had to go to work for a bank when she graduated from high school, so she did. Valerie's life was fenced in by very small boundaries at that time. She worked a lot of hours at the bank, and when she wasn't working, she was working out. Her vacations were spent at her home; she never traveled anywhere. Her grandparents had always told her to work hard, save her money, and balance her checkbook to the penny. When she got laid off after thirteen years working in the banking industry, Valerie had all this free time and she had money in the bank. Why not buy a motorcycle?

Valerie's friend drove the new motorcycle home for her and she took it out for a few short rides. Three months later, it was just sitting there. Valerie thought, "That was sure a horrible investment—I just bought a bucket of bolts and it's just sitting there taking up space." Then one day a friend mentioned he was going for a ride and she asked,

203

"What kind of ride?" He told her about riding motorcycles and she said, "I have a bike!" He said, "No, you don't!" And Valerie said, "Yes, I do!" He was part of a mostly male group of ten to fifteen people who rode together. Valerie asked if she could ride with them and was told she had to ride and keep up or just stay at home. She had only been on her bike about six times and really had to push the limits of her comfort zone. The group was riding fast and Valerie hit some loose gravel by the freeway and a tire got loose, which she describes as 'like driving on ice when you're on a bike.' After that experience she decided to drive her own pace from point 'A' to point 'B' when riding with them and get there safely.

"Motorcycles changed my entire life!" Valerie exclaimed. "I traveled to Arizona for bike week and went to Sturgis and Laughlin. I had never traveled on my vacations, and I was seeing new places and having new experiences. I wanted to see more." She fell in love with Scottsdale, Arizona, the first time she came and told all of her friends her goal was to live there, but it had to be close to Fashion Square Mall. Shopping for unique items is her very favorite thing to do.

Valerie took a job at the Harley Davidson dealership in Seattle, and often found herself helping people select parts for their new bikes. She ripped pictures out of magazines when she designed her own bike. With advice and help from her friends, she selected the rims, the seats, the mirrors, the handlebars and added lots of chrome. She pictured in her mind exactly what the bike would look like. Since business at the dealership was seasonal, she had the flexibility to take time off, and returned to Scottsdale in 2004 for the Arizona Bike Week. Her friends encouraged her to stay. After house-sitting their condo for three months in the sweltering Arizona summer, she decided to buy a condo and move to Scottsdale.

Valerie describes herself as very shy and she knew few people in Scottsdale. When her biker friends came to town, they went to the places where other bikers hung out and she began to build a circle of friends she could ride with. "Next thing you know we're all racing down Scottsdale Road. I still had my 'Fat Boy' and they would always try to keep me in the back." Then one day when we got to the restaurant, a friend said to me "Valerie, you are out of control. Take it to the racetrack." Valerie said "I felt about an inch tall right then. I looked around and realized we were all out of control. They were getting speeding tickets and I didn't want one, so I did take it to the racetrack."

"I fell in love with the track and began racing. At the ten day event in Sturgis, the owner of Hacienda Harley Davidson called me and said, "If I buy this bike, will you race it for us?" After excitedly shouting, 'yes', Valerie realized that this was going to require a lot of money. She had no experience putting together marketing packages or sponsorship proposals and was very uncomfortable calling people to ask for financial support for an 'upcoming female racer' who had yet to become a champion.

"Google was my best friend ever! I learned a great deal and did my own research during my quest for sponsors. My very first sponsor was Monster Energy Drink. When I finally got in to see the guy, he told me he didn't know why he hadn't agreed earlier since I was so persistent. I still have the very first can of Monster Drink that they gave me, and I will keep it forever because it symbolizes the turning point in my life."

"I didn't know I had all of this creativity and courage in me," Valerie shared as she ventured into a new world of sponsored racing. "I was so shy, and I was skinny and people called me Popeye; they said I would blow away in the wind. I wore long sleeves so people couldn't see my arms." Hours and hours at the gym paid off for Valerie and she is now well muscled and up to the challenge of racing in the big leagues on a big bike. She attributes her efforts of transforming her body to the confidence she has today.

"I can do anything!" Valerie has an unshakeable belief in herself, and said, "I told everyone I was going to be a Pro Stock Motorcycle Racer!" She ignored the negative input from people who didn't think she could do it. Racing requires total commitment. She cannot have a job during the week and race on the weekend. She must be "all in" all the time and focused on her goals. "I found that passion in me to do everything I wanted to do and needed to do to be successful," Valerie shared. "I sold my BMW convertible to buy the truck and trailer I needed to transport my bike to the races!"

"I always listened to advice," Valerie emphasized when talking about her success. That willingness to listen impacts her personal life as well. Valerie asks another friend racing on the circuit, "How do you handle all of it . . . the autographs, the loneliness of the road trips, the glamour, and the fans?" Taking his advice, she decided to get a 'purse dog'. Reckon, a totally lovable Maltese, now travels everywhere with Valerie and keeps a smile on her face.

One of the greatest obstacles Valerie faced was being given great equipment and not knowing what to do with it. "I knew I couldn't fail . . . I had to learn how to be perfect at what I was doing. I was persistent, I researched, and I learned fast."

"Be open. You never know when you will discover your passion. I didn't know I was built for speed. I was working in a bank! I got the message the day someone told me to 'take it to the track.' "

Racing is only one of Valerie's passions. She loves her volunteer work with HopeKids, an organization dedicated to restoring hope and transforming the lives of children with serious illness. She loves baking and cupcakes, and can envision herself in retail, or maybe breeding dogs is a future possibility.

Looking to the future, Valerie is going back to Bonneville Flats with her sights on setting new records. "I've got a new racing sponsor," Valerie announced! "I'm back."

"People who cannot invent and reinvent themselves must be content with borrowed postures, secondhand ideas, fitting in instead of standing out."
— *Warren G. Bennis*

REINVENTING YOUR BUSINESS

Insanity: Doing the same thing over and over and expecting a different result. If you are struggling to understand why you are not moving forward in your life or your business, it is time to take a closer look at what you are doing. Today's world moves fast! To stay ahead of your competition, you must be totally tuned in to your market and ready to adapt to new demands and new opportunities. The economy has forced many people to completely reinvent their careers and their businesses. Opportunities abound which allow you to leave behind unsatisfying jobs and explore the career or business that has been a forgotten dream. Now is the time to make it a reality.

Debbie Allen Is the Queen of Reinvention

"What I was doing in my business was no longer working," says Debbie Allen, international keynote speaker, author of *Confessions of Shameless Self Promoters,* and president of Debbie Allen International. "The economic situation cut the speaking opportunities in half. I was facing some personal struggles; I felt stuck and kept hitting walls. I knew I had to make massive innovations in my business, but it just wasn't coming together. I had to ask myself, 'Why isn't it working? How am I communicating? Where are the opportunities?' I am NOT giving up on my dream! I knew I just had to find a different way of doing it. When you are swimming in the sea of sameness, you must search for a different path." It was time for Debbie to reinvent the business that had stalled.

Debbie was an experienced businesswoman and an expert in the field of marketing. A lifelong entrepreneur, Debbie describes her defining moment happening at age thirty when she made a decision to go out on her own in business. She grew up in Gary, Indiana, and had been working in her family's business for many years. She owned part of the business which she bought into at age nineteen, but she had no passion for it. She knew there had to be something else out there that didn't feel like a "JOB"! Debbie was looking for the next opportunity. Her mother owned a small nine-hundred-square-foot clothing store for six years, but it wasn't making any money. So with no job, no college degree, and no retail experience, Debbie bought the business. When the 'dream stealers' in her life stepped in to voice their opinions, she refused to let them get in her way. In fact, their negativity encouraged her to continue on her path to prove she could be successful. She wanted to make 100% of all the decisions. Unfortunately, "I also made 100% of all the mistakes. It was very challenging," Debbie said, "but in two and one half years, I took this business from making no profit to a multi-million dollar business."

From the beginning Debbie wanted her business to "have her stamp on it." The fashion industry was exciting; she traveled to New York five times a year and made frequent trips to Los Angeles. She learned "you can actually make money doing something you love," and could also help women look and feel good about themselves at the same time. Helping women succeed inspired Debbie then and continues to inspire and motivate her today.

I asked Debbie how she was able to achieve her initial success in the retail business, and she was very quick to tell me she always found mentors. She asked people for their support and help to increase her knowledge, and she was willing to pay them just for talking to her. She joined what today would be called a mastermind group with people who had fifteen to thirty years' experience in retail, and learned everything she could about the industry. Debbie says, "It's insanity to learn a business by yourself when others know how to do it." She studied, she learned, and she became an expert.

Debbie doesn't always enjoy running a business at its pinnacle. She thrives while building a business and then says, "What's next?" She describes herself as a 'true entrepreneur' with a strong sense of independence and innovation. She knew the retail industry inside out, and when she recognized a need for speakers at retail industry events, she made a decision to start speaking and training. What most people didn't know about Debbie was the fact that she was very shy as a young person and forced herself to take public speaking in high school. She joined Toastmasters to increase her ability to communicate well as she networked for her business. She always won competitively when giving prepared speeches, but says she was terrible at impromptu talks. Being prepared was very important to her. She said having a goal and knowing your topic well takes away your nervousness.

"Choosing to go into speaking was my greatest business success," says Debbie. "It allowed me to be able to touch many more lives and to go international."

We talked about Debbie's success and she shared that people frequently say, "I want to do what you do!" Debbie defines success as "when you make it look easy." She does make it look easy, but that doesn't happen overnight. Debbie may not have a traditional college degree, but she has expert business knowledge that she paid many thousands of dollars to acquire through personal and business mentors and coaches. After ten years speaking in the retail industry, Debbie began headlining and giving keynote speeches. She then niched into boot camp speaking and training. Today Debbie is recognized as a marketing expert and speaks internationally. Her successful reinvention as "The Millionaire Entrepreneur Business Builder" and her collaboration with others led her to a highly successful worldwide speaking tour. Being an international traveler with a great sense of adventure taught Debbie compassion about other cultures, a trait valuable to her as she works in an international marketplace. She now describes herself as a citizen of the world.

"Be true to yourself and don't give up who you really are," advises Debbie. "Never give up, and do all you can to build your confidence and self-esteem. Get out of your comfort zone every day. There are no shortcuts!" Debbie firmly believes that taking risks is part of being an entrepreneur, and you become empowered when you push beyond your fears. To gain immediate success and move to a higher level more rapidly, she recommends creating supportive alliances and aligning yourself with the right social and business partners.

Debbie wants her legacy to be "I helped thousands of people worldwide to achieve their passion and get the success they DESERVE!"

Debbie is living her dream career, and she wants women around the world to hear her message and believe they can do it too.

SECTION IV

YOUR JOURNEY BEGINS HERE

"The world has the habit of making room for the man whose words and actions show that he knows where he is going."
    — *Napoleon Hill*

DEVELOP YOUR PLAN

You have just shared the unbelievable stories of women who overcame seemingly insurmountable obstacles and shattered barriers to achieve their personal dreams. Each woman made a decision at a defining moment in her life to move in a specific direction toward a future she envisioned for herself. Reaching that decision was indeed a monumental turning point, but making it happen required a plan of action.

Many people dream great dreams of what they want in their life, but very few actually succeed. That is because most people do not set specific goals and take the time to develop an actual plan to achieve their goals. It is simple; it is not always easy.

You can chose to succeed by deciding what you want to accomplish in your life, by writing down your goals, and developing precise, step-by-step activities to achieve them. Your goals must be crystal clear. Just saying "I want to be rich, I want to own a business," or "I want to travel," is not enough. You must decide exactly how much money you want to make, what type of business you want to own, or which countries you want to explore. To begin, you must write down your goals and read them every day. Then brainstorm to determine exactly what steps you must take to make your goals a reality.

Start by developing very detailed steps that will guide your actions as you progress toward your goal. This business plan or life plan becomes your roadmap for your personal journey.

"Ordinary people believe only in the possible. Extraordinary people visualize not what is possible or probable, but rather what is impossible. And by visualizing the impossible, they begin to see it as possible."
— Cherie Carter-Scott

VISUALIZE YOUR SUCCESS!

Start living your new life right now! You don't have to wait for the reality of that life to manifest itself. Visualization is the key to success in everything. This powerful tool allows your subconscious mind to take over and guide you toward your goals because it cannot distinguish between truth and fiction. You have the ability to program your mind by consistently playing movies in your mind of the future you want. Do it in full color and with strong emotion. See and feel yourself in the role you desire for your future. If your visualization is powerful enough, you only have to catch up in time.

Write positive affirmations describing yourself in your new role. An excellent example is to repeat over and over "I am a confident and successful woman. I am excited each day as I write another chapter in my book." Make a commitment to yourself to affirm and visualize your new life daily. Visualize yourself exactly as you described it in *your* story. Do it every morning when you wake and every evening right before you go to sleep.

Successful people around the world understand and utilize this proven technique in every area of their life . . . business, personal, financial, physical, emotional, and spiritual . . . to rewrite their future. They design their dream life, and step-by-step travel along their personal journey to their intended destination.

"You don't have to be great to get started, but you have to get started to be great."

— *Les Brown*

TAKE ACTION

Do it now! No time will ever be better than right now to get started. Excuses only make you feel guilty.

Waiting for the perfect conditions, the perfect opportunity, or the perfect time wastes your life. It's so easy to procrastinate and find other things to do in today's world. Our cell phones have become an extension of our hand and are always within reach. When the red light flashes, we cannot resist checking it immediately. New emails constantly arrive, and we think we must respond at once. But staying focused on a project without any outside distractions is the most time efficient way to work and will move you closer to your goals.

Develop a system that works for you. Create a list of daily action items and prioritize your list. Which items are most important to your goal attainment? Do those first! Effective people love the thrill of getting things done.

Journal and review your progress daily and make necessary adjustments. Now is not the time to falter. You know where you want to go and how you need to get there. Step boldly onto your path.

"The future is not something that just happens to you. The future is something you do."

— *Glen Hiemstra*

BUILDING THE FUTURE . . . YOUR LEGACY

"Women Will Rule the World" was the title of an article published in Newsweek Magazine, July 6, 2010. These are extremely powerful words and herald a major shift in our world. The article said, *". . . like the reality that, because it's women, not men, who are starting businesses of their own, it will be women, not men, who will one day employ a majority of workers. As with most trends involving female empowerment, the shift has begun in the US and is emanating outward."*

The new roles created by this change will bring about many opportunities for women to distinguish themselves as leaders and business owners. Large business or small, successful women of the future must be unique in their approach to business and leadership.

"A remarkable trend is emerging in the U.S. job market--one that will greatly impact the workplace of tomorrow. Women are becoming the nation's job-creation engine, starting small businesses and stimulating new jobs at a rate that outdistances their male counterparts and disproportionately exceeds their current contribution

to U.S. employment. A newly published report by The Guardian Life Small Business Research Institute projects that female-owned small businesses, now just 16% of total U.S. employment, will be responsible for creating one-third of the 15.3 million new jobs anticipated by the Bureau of Labor Statistics by 2018." (Forbes, January 12, 2010)

Current economic challenges in our country and the world have forced many people who have lost jobs, or been forced by individual circumstances to enter the workforce to look for new ventures. This has not only opened opportunities for creativity, it also allows people to explore occupations in areas where they have a passion. In many cases, people are going into business for themselves and are reaching for their dreams. The opportunities for women are boundless.

Whether you are searching for a way to advance in the corporate world, escape the corporate world, have more flexibility in your life by being your own boss, or launch the company you have long envisioned, now is the time to realize the dream you have for your business, your career, and your life.

Discover your dream, create your legacy, and love your journey. Join the ranks of women around the world who have journeyed to personal empowerment, and support other women traveling their own personal path to empowerment.

United in support of others, we will make a difference in our world!

LEARN MORE ABOUT
THESE AMAZING WOMEN

Clarissa Burt: Clarissa Burt Media Group, www.ClarissaBurt.com; www.Facebook.com/ClarissaBurt-Official

Carina Prescott: Lucid Valuations and Investments, Inc., www.Lucidvaluations.com; www.Facebook.com/LucidValuations.

Dana Morgan-Hovind: Owner/Designer, D Mo Apparel, LLC; www.dmobaby.com; www.Facebook.com/D-mo-baby.

Miranda: Red Carpet Extravaganza, www.Facebook.com/RedCarpetExtravaganza; Circle of Helping Hands, www.COHH.org.

Jyl Steinback: Shape Up US, Inc., www.ShapeUpUS.org, www.AmericasHealthiestMom.com; www.Facebook.com/JylSteinback.

Gia Heller: The National Business Experts, www.TheNationalBusinessExperts.com; www.Facebook.com/TheNationalBusinessExperts.

Christina Wagner: www.Facebook.com/ChristinaWagner; www.Facebook.com/votvaz.

LeAnn Hull: Commissioner, Phoenix Sister Cities; Arizona Window Center, www.Facebook.com/LeAnnHull.

Nicole Angeline: Crazy in Heels, www.CrazyInHeels.net; www.Facebook.com/CrazyInHeelsBiPolar.

Kassey Frazier: www.KasseyFrazier.com; www.Facebook.com/KasseyFrazier.

Joan Spalding: New Options for Learning, www.NewOptionsForLearning.com; www.SpaldingTrees.com.

CiCi Berardi: You Go Boy Marketing, www.YouGoBoyAZ.com; www.Facebook.com/CiCiYougoboyaz; www.Facebook.com/CiCiFessupBarbie.

Marsha Petrie Sue: Marsha Petrie Sue, www.MarshaPetrieSue.com. www.Facebook.com/MarshaPetrieSue.

Pam Gaber: Gabriel's Angels, www.GabrielsAngels.org; www.Facebook.com/GabrielsAngels.

Michelle Medrano: New Vision Spiritual Growth Center, www.NewVisionAZ.org; www.Facebook.com/MichelleMedrano.

Sally Horton Kelley: Sally is a physician specializing in Obstetrics & Gynecology.

Kyna Rosen: Get Fit with Kyna, www.GetFitWithKyna.com; www.KangooClubAZ.com; www.GetFitWKyna.blogspot.com.

Holly Hunter: Founder AZ Active Kids, www.AZActiveKids.com; www.meetup.com/The-Active-AZ-Families-meetup-group.

Gelie Akhenblit: NetworkingPhoenix.com, www.NetworkingPhoenix.com; www.Facebook.com/NetworkingPhoenix.

Janet Brooks: Janet Brooks Designs, www.JanetBrooksDesigns.com; www.Facebook.com/JanetBrooksDesign.

Marie O'Riordan: iDealBusinessSolutions, www.iDealBusinessSolutions.com; www.MarieORiordanInternational.com; www.Facebook.com/MarieORiordanInternational.

Kimber Leigh: www.Facebook.com/kimberaleigh; imdb.com/name/nm1971718/.

Julie Armstrong: Phoenix Job Corps, Community Liaison/Workforce Integration.

Tracy Repchuk: Power Business Mentors International., LLC; www.MillionaireByDesign.com.

Debbie Allen: Debbie Allen International, www.DebbieAllen.com; www.PowerBusinessMentors.com.

Valerie Thompson: Valerie Thompson Racing, www.ValerieThompsonRacing.com; www.Facebook.com/ValerieThompsonRacing.

About the Author

Dolores Seright, the Sales Training Expert for Professional Women, is a professional speaker, sales trainer and coach. She successfully trained, mentored and coached many people during her twenty-year career in the pharmaceutical industry. During that career she was highly successful as a sales representative and received many national awards year after year, including the prestigious President's Club, as a top-performing salesperson and, later as a sales manager. She consistently advanced in her career to higher level positions, including corporate sales trainer, district sales manager, division manager and regional business director. For her, it's been an exciting journey discovering her personal dreams and turning them into reality!

Dolores faced a personal challenge with a breast cancer diagnosis, and made a decision to work full time while undergoing chemotherapy and radiation treatments. She and her region were committed to success, and they achieved the #1 ranking in her division under her leadership. She is dedicated to teaching others skills they can utilize for a lifetime.

Dolores is a certified professional coach, and her passion is teaching women the skills to move beyond the obstacles holding them back from achieving their personal and business success. She has learned the value of mentors and personal coaches to navigate through the corporate environment. Through focus and dedication, she was able to achieve tremendous success in her sales career and, as a single mother, financially support her family. She has had the experience of being a small business owner and is uniquely able to understand the challenges faced by business owners who are struggling to take their business to a higher level. She discovered a passion for coaching others and teaching them the skills to achieve their potential and succeed in their careers or business. She made a decision to leave the corporate world to pursue her personal dream of training, coaching and mentoring others. Dolores is an experienced coach and specializes in teaching selling strategies and skills to women. She also speaks and facilitates workshops on many topics.

Dolores also believes in the importance of giving back to the community and volunteers as a career coach and conducts training workshops at Fresh Start Women's Foundation.

Her mission is to coach women to achieve success in their career or business by learning not only to sell . . . but to excel!

Dolores Teaches Women to Sell . . . and Excel

In *"Shattering Barriers,"* Dolores Seright shares techniques and strategies for personal empowerment for all women. Her mission is to coach women to achieve success in their career or business by learning not only to sell . . . but to excel!

Her enthusiasm, knowledge and passion team up to make her a dynamite speaker for a wide range of audiences. To discuss hiring her as a speaker for your next event, contact her office at 480-518-3504, international 1+480-518-3504, or from her website at www.WomenWhoSellExcel.com.

Presentation Topics Include:
- Shattering Your Personal Barriers
- Solution Driven Selling That Allows You to Excel
- Developing an Attitude of Success

Want to Learn More Strategies to Excel?

Keep up to date on Dolores' webinars, seminars and additional resources. Sign up for your free report "The 7 Secrets to Powerhouse Selling" and receive Dolores' six week eCourse bonus at www.WomenWhoSellExcel.com.

Contact Information:

Women Who Sell Excel, LLC

P O Box 18789

Fountain Hills, AZ 85269

Phone: 480-518-3504; International: 1+ 480-518-3504

Email: Dolores@WomenWhoSellExcel.com

Website: www.WomenWhoSellExcel.com

Blog: www.DoloresSeright.com